D1017253

LIBRARY *of* GREAT AUTHORS

SPARK
NOTES

LIBRARY *of* GREAT AUTHORS

Albert Camus
Lewis Carroll
Fyodor Dostoevsky
Barbara Kingsolver
Gabriel García Márquez
Toni Morrison
Vladimir Nabokov
J.K. Rowling
J.R.R. Tolkien
Virginia Woolf

SPARK
NOTES

LIBRARY *of* GREAT AUTHORS

Vladimir Nabokov

His Life and Works

Stanley P. Baldwin

EDITORIAL DIRECTOR Justin Kestler
EXECUTIVE EDITOR Ben Florman
SERIES EDITOR Emma Chastain

INTERIOR DESIGN Dan Williams

Produced by The Wonderland Press and published by SparkNotes

Spark Publishing
A Division of SparkNotes LLC
120 5th Avenue
New York, NY 10011

10 9 8 7 6 5 4 3 2 1

Please submit comments or questions, or report errors to www.sparknotes.com/errors

Printed and bound in the United States of America

ISBN 1-58663-842-4

Cover photograph Copyright © 2003 by Corbis, Inc.

Library of Congress Cataloging-in-Publication Data available on request

Contents

Contents

$$\left\{ \begin{array}{c} \text{III.} \\ \text{Pnin} \\ 51 \end{array} \right\}$$

$$\left\{ \begin{array}{c} \text{IV.} \\ \text{Pale Fire} \\ 89 \end{array} \right\}$$

Contents

{ Topics In Depth }

The

LIBRARY *of* GREAT AUTHORS

series explores the intimate connection between writing and experience, shedding light on the work of literature's most esteemed authors by examining their lives. The complete LIBRARY *of* GREAT AUTHORS brings an excitingly diverse crowd to your bookshelf, from Fyodor Dostoevsky to J.K. Rowling.

Each book in the LIBRARY *of* GREAT AUTHORS features full-length analysis of the writer's most famous works, including such novels as *Crime and Punishment, Lolita, The Lord of the Rings,* and *Mrs. Dalloway.* Whether you are a reader craving deeper knowledge of your favorite author, a student studying the classics, or a new convert to a celebrated novel, turn to the LIBRARY *of* GREAT AUTHORS for thorough, fascinating, and insightful coverage of literature's best writers.

SPARK
NOTES

LIBRARY *of* GREAT AUTHORS

Vladimir
Nabokov

I

THE LIFE OF VLADIMIR NABOKOV

One of the world's most inventive writers of lyric and satirical prose, raising the eyebrows even of highbrows with his 1955 novel *Lolita*, **Vladimir Nabokov** was born in St. Petersburg, Russia, on April 23, 1899. The future author's father, **V. D. Nabokov** (1870–1922), was a very wealthy man, and if you were wealthy and living in Russia during the reign of **Tsar Nicholas II** (1868–1918), you enjoyed privilege and abundance. Already a respected minor politician at the age of twenty-seven, Nabokov's father married **Elena Rukavishnikov** (1876–1939), an heiress whose family owned a lumber business and gold mines in Siberia. The Nabokovs' large pink-granite home was a salon for world-famous intellectuals, musicians, poets, and bankers. Its walls displayed the works of well-known artists. The Nabokov family, their friends, and even their servants spoke French, English, and Russian.

For a young boy fond of reading, Vladimir Nabokov had an idyllic childhood. The family library was vast, and his French and English tutors were highly qualified. When asked about his early childhood, Nabokov said, tongue in cheek, he had enjoyed "a perfectly normal trilingual childhood in a family with a large library." After the Nabokovs enrolled Vladimir at the exclusive Tenishev School, they hired a chauffeur to drive him to and from classes in one of St. Petersburg's few black Rolls-Royce limousines.

Not surprisingly, the other children thought Vladimir was a bit of a snob, especially since he wrote poetry and hunted butterflies. However, he was a tenacious goalkeeper for the school's soccer team, a role that won him the friendship and respect of his classmates.

When Vladimir was sixteen years old, his beloved **Uncle Ruka** (1874–1916) gave him an astonishing birthday gift: a large estate and the equivalent of two million dollars. One of Vladimir's first extravagances was to pay for the private publication of a book of his poems in a 500-copy edition. A few months later, however, Tsar Nicholas II abdicated, and life took a bad turn for the Nabokovs. The Bolsheviks, a revolutionary faction of the Communist Party, seized control of the government, and soldiers confiscated the estates of many rich and politically suspect families, so the Nabokovs fled St. Petersburg, taking only a few handfuls of jewelry with them. The Russian Revolution (1917–1921) had begun.

Vladimir Nabokov

The Russian Revolution: Like many revolutions, the Russian Revolution was born of unrest, poverty, and despair. While Tsar Nicholas II and his family sailed on their luxury yacht, peasants were starving. In Petrograd and Moscow, workers were striking and rioting for higher food rations. Soldiers understood poverty, because they were underpaid—when they were paid at all—and they sometimes refused to suppress the insurgents. Military insubordination and a mutinous spirit spread, and organized rioters took over the capital in St. Petersburg in 1917. Nicholas was forced to abdicate, and professional people and government workers escaped to neighboring countries in fear of being punished alongside those zealously loyal to the tsar. Because Nabokov's father had held minor government posts, the family immediately fled the country, taking only what they could wear and carry.

> "Much as I like owning a Rolls-Royce, I could do without it. What I could not do without is a typewriter."
>
> **JOHN O'HARA**

The Nabokovs struggled with desperate poverty. They settled in Yalta, traveled to Constantinople, and from there went to England, where Vladimir and his brother **Sergi** (1900–1945) qualified for émigré scholarships and enrolled in Cambridge in 1919. V.D. and Elena Nabokov then moved to Berlin, where V.D. became editor of a small Russian-language newspaper. Three years later, during a political lecture, he was killed in an outburst of gunfire meant to assassinate the speaker.

After graduating from Cambridge in 1922, Nabokov settled in Berlin and worked at a variety of jobs—movie extra, tennis coach, translator, and tutor. Occasionally, he published short pieces of fiction and some poetry. He kept busy playing soccer and giving public readings of his fiction, trying to ward off depression. He had lost his father, and he had lost Russia, his homeland.

In 1925, when Nabokov was twenty-six, he married **Véra Slonim** (1902–1991), another Russian émigré. The following year, he published his first novel, *Mashenka (Mary)*. Written in Russian, it tells the story of a young émigré and the girl he left behind in Russia. During the next twelve years, Nabokov completed several plays and published dozens of short stories and eight more novels, all in Russian. He was highly respected in Berlin's Russian literary circles, but money was scarce, especially for writers. Inflation and unemployment ran rampant in Germany, despite the promises of Germany's *Führer*, **Adolf Hitler** (1889–1945).

The Life of Vladimir Nabokov

A *Führer* Comes to Power: When Adolf Hitler gained power in Germany, he immediately turned his malevolence on Jewish people. He addressed Germans on the radio and in newsreels, telling them the Jews were responsible for their country's desperate economic depression. Hitler claimed he would solve his country's economic problems, but only if he had the freedom to deal with the Jews as he saw fit. Beginning in 1933, Germany's Jews became second-class citizens. Their shops were boycotted, they were required to wear yellow cloth stars, and they had to use separate parks. This shameful treatment was the first step in what turned into the most horrifying state-sponsored mass murder in human history. Jews were forced into ghettos and eventually loaded into cattle cars and sent to concentration camps, where they were gassed, worked to death, or murdered in some other way. In the end, Hitler caused the deaths of over six million Jews.

As Hitler's regime flourished, revolution was in the air, but both Vladimir and his Jewish wife, Véra, did their best to ignore what was happening. Book burnings had begun, and the Nazis had marched into the Rhineland. The 1936 Olympic games in Berlin were an exercise in Nazi glorification. Unlike the Nabokovs, many intellectuals and writers feared Hitler's fanaticism. In all, over 2,000 writers, scientists, and artists left Germany. Most of them settled in the United States. Nabokov and his family stayed on, remaining in Berlin until 1937, when Nabokov learned that Hitler had released his father's killer from prison and made him supervisor of emigration. Véra insisted that the family leave at once.

After settling in Paris, Nabokov wrote his first novel in English, *The Real Life of Sebastian Knight* (1941), in his converted study—a sunny bathroom. He wrote most of the novel there, using a suitcase placed across a bidet as his desk. Money was even tighter in Paris than it had been in Berlin because no one was interested in hiring an English tutor who was Russian.

By 1940, the German army was threatening Paris with invasion, and Nabokov was convinced that his future lay in America, where he had been hired to teach two courses of modern Russian literature at Stanford University for the 1941 summer term. The Nabokovs sailed for New York. From there, a friend drove them to California, stopping along the way in Tennessee, Texas, and Arizona so Vladimir and Véra could hunt butterflies.

Nabokov's lectures at Stanford were popular, and, in his free time, he wrote and played chess. He next found employment at Wellesley College in Massachusetts, where he taught no regular courses but gave six lectures a year. In the meantime, he forced himself to compose fiction in English and frequently visited Harvard's Museum of Comparative Zoology, where he helped catalogue the butterfly collection.

Vladimir Nabokov

In America: In 1945, Nabokov made two major changes in his life: he gave up his four-pack-a-day cigarette habit, and he became an American citizen. Three years later, he began teaching at Cornell University, in Ithaca, New York. He would stay there as a professor of Russian and European literature for ten years. During summers, Nabokov and Véra hunted butterflies in the Rocky Mountains, and he began writing chapters of *Pnin* (1953), a comic portrait of an aging, endearing European professor of Russian literature at a small American college. Véra sent single chapters to *The New Yorker*, hoping for quick sales so they could pay bills. The magazine bought the chapters, edited them lightly—to Nabokov's horror—and published them at intervals.

> "Nabokov writes prose the only way it should be written, that is, ecstatically."
>
> **JOHN UPDIKE**, *THE NEW YORKER*

Nabokov also began fashioning the novel that would stun the Western world when Paris's Olympia Press published it in 1955: *Lolita*, the story of a thirty-seven-year-old man's obsession with his twelve-year-old stepdaughter. Nabokov had attempted to sell the manuscript to several U.S. publishers, but they all refused, calling it lewd and scandalous, a "time bomb" waiting to explode.

In 1958, three years after *Lolita* had been published in Europe to financial success and critical acclaim, it was published in the U.S., where it remained on the bestseller list for over six months, in part because of its notoriety. Many public libraries banned it, and the *Chicago Tribune* refused to review it.

In 1961, Nabokov moved to Montreux, Switzerland, where he began translating all of his Russian novels into English. He also produced two additional masterworks: *Pale Fire* (1962), a long narrative poem accompanied by copious, fussy notes; and *Ada* (1968), a family chronicle filled with tragic interludes and daring romances. Critics in Europe and the U.S. were quick to lavish praise on both of these novels. Nabokov, weary of being hounded by boring reviewers, said, "I don't fish, cook, dance, endorse books, sign books, co-sign declarations, eat oysters, get drunk . . . I'm an old mild gentleman, very kind." Nabokov died July 2, 1977, of a viral infection that had spread to his lungs.

People, Events, and Trends

That Influenced Nabokov's Work

A Baby Boom: The late 1940s and 1950s in America were characterized by a spirit of exuberance and consumerism. World War II was over. American participation had shortened the war, and the surviving soldiers came home and started fathering babies, producing the Baby Boomer generation. People wanted to move out of the cities and into the suburbs. Throughout the U.S., cookie-cutter houses sprung up in identical patterns. They were mass-produced and affordable, and few people seemed to care that their dream home looked just like all the others on the block. With the migration to the newly built suburbs, new expressways and freeways were built to handle commuter traffic. Electric clothes washers replaced old crank models, and everyone wanted phones in their home and a new car in the garage. Veterans filled the nation's colleges and universities on the G. I. Bill.

Faster Life, Faster Food: American life picked up pace. McDonald's restaurants sprang up across the country, offering fast burgers and fries for low prices. Innovations such as Reddi-Whip were introduced in supermarkets, freeing women from a few of the long hours that kitchen work claimed. V-8 juice gave orange juice a run for its money. Prepackaged cake mixes were introduced, along with Minute Rice products. Tupperware containers revolutionized food storage. Instead of old-fashioned, healthy breakfast cereals like Wheaties and Post Toasties, kids wanted Sugar Smacks and Sugar Frosted Flakes.

Hot Cars: Tailfins were the rage on the road, and there seemed no end to their length and stylistic innovations. Some tailfins were almost half as high as the cars they adorned. Cars during the thirties and early forties were unexciting, but after the war, consumers demanded "dream cars," hot rods and sports cars. Neighborhoods crawled with brand-new MGs, Alfa Romeos, Porsches, and Triumphs.

Vladimir Nabokov

Toys and Television: Children began playing with plastic toys; wooden and metal toys suddenly seemed old-fashioned. Silly Putty fascinated children and adults, and the Davy Crockett craze spawned a demand for fur caps with raccoon tails. Hula hoops whirled around hips and Barbie dolls redefined female beauty for generations of adolescents. Kids watched *Howdy Doody*, and their parents watched Ed Sullivan's *Toast of the Town* or *The Lone Ranger*. Young and old knew the words to the theme song of the *Mickey Mouse Club*. At the movies, people lined up to see Marilyn Monroe, James Dean, and 3-D extravaganzas.

Polio Vaccine and Elvis: In the mid-1950s, the polio vaccine Jonas Salk developed was administered to most of the nation's children. In a few years, polio was eradicated. In 1957, the Russians launched *Sputnik*, and the space race was on. At about the same time, Bill Haley and the Comets burst forth with a theme for music of the fifties—music that would shake, rattle, and roll. They were followed by Elvis Presley, who ruled pop music throughout the era.

Nabokov's Literary Context

His Influences and Impact

Vladimir Nabokov is an acknowledged master of English prose, a remarkable title by any standard, and especially so since Nabokov grew up speaking and writing Russian as his primary language.

One facet of Nabokov's mastery is his punning wit. His style is frequently compared to that of modernist literary innovator **James Joyce** (1882–1941). Nabokov puns, uses alliteration and assonance, mingles French idioms with American legalese, and makes abundant reference to American cultural symbols.

Lolita, though transparently a tale of sexual obsession, can also be read as a twentieth-century update of the satiric travel narrative, a form most notably employed by writers **Geoffrey Chaucer** (c.1343–1400) and **Jonathan Swift** (1667–1745). In the same way that Chaucer and Swift shocked (and angered) their audiences with irreverent characterizations of clergy and government, Nabokov subverted the prim suburban sensibility that characterized post-war America by portraying a sexual affair between a man and a child.

While Nabokov's novels are often classed with twentieth-century American novels, his Russian heritage makes him an atypical American novelist, especially because he clashed with the conformist culture of the 1950s. Nabokov's important American writing influences, like the author himself, were not typical of mainstream America. One of his favorite authors was the American poet and short-story writer **Edgar Allan Poe** (1809–1849), famous for his gothic tales of mystery and dread. Nabokov was also fascinated by the American writers **Washington Irving** (1783–1859), **Herman Melville** (1819–1891), **Nathaniel Hawthorne** (1804–1864), and **Henry James** (1843–1916). He belongs to the group of Russian masters that includes **Alexander Pushkin** (1799–1837), **Fyodor Dostoevsky** (1821–1881), and **Leo Tolstoy** (1828–1910).

II

LOLITA

Lolita

An Overview

Key Facts

Genre: Satiric tragi-comedy

Date of First Publication: 1955, Paris; 1958, New York

Setting: The late 1940s and early 1950s; the New England towns of Ramsdale and Beardsley; the roads of the United States.

Narrator: Humbert Humbert, in the first person.

Plot Overview: Thirty-seven-year-old Humbert Humbert falls in love with his landlady's twelve-year-old daughter, Lolita. He marries the landlady, who is soon killed in an automobile accident. Humbert initiates a sexual relationship with Lolita, takes her on a year-long driving tour, settles with her for a while in a New England town, and then takes her on the road again. Eventually, Lolita slips away with a man who has been following them. Five years later, Humbert tracks down Lolita's abductor, Clare Quilty, and kills him. Humbert writes *Lolita* from his cell, awaiting trial for Quilty's murder.

Vladimir Nabokov

Style, Technique, and Language

Style—Humor in Unlikely Places: Nabokov has a gift for humor and a sense that the world is mad. Although *Lolita* can be considered a tragedy, it is also a comedy. Nabokov takes scenes that could be horrifying or sad or merely sexual, and makes them absurd and hilarious. Humbert pokes fun at himself, using the overblown language of romance novels to describe mundane moments. For example, when explaining what happened when he was thirteen and full of passion for twelve-year-old Annabel Leigh, instead of saying baldly that he handed Annabel his penis, he says he handed her "the scepter of [his] passion."

> "*Lolita* is one of our finest American novels, a triumph of style and vision, an unforgettable work, Nabokov's best (though not most characteristic) work, a wedding of Swiftian satirical vigor with the kind of minute, loving patience that belongs to a man infatuated with the visual mysteries of the world."
>
> JOYCE CAROL OATES, NABOKOV:
> A CENTENARY CELEBRATION

Technique—A Confession and a Mystery: Nabokov frames the novel with a foreword that parodies both legalese and prudish people who hide their lust with primness. Nabokov presents this novel as a long confessional document, not a novel, a premise he bolsters by alternating straightforward prose with such things as Humbert's journal entries, Lolita's class roll list, a postcard from Camp Q, and a letter from John Farlow. Not only confession, *Lolita*'s second half is a mystery. Nabokov makes a detective story out of the wanderings of Humbert and Lolita, as Humbert wonders about the identity of the mysterious man who tracks the couple.

Language—A *Tour de Force*: In *Lolita*, lust and violence are secondary to Nabokov's pyrotechnic *tour de force* performance in the English language. His prose, at times breathless and filled with alliteration and assonance, often slows and takes on a grandeur. Nabokov enjoys toying with the possibilities of the multilingual mishmash of the English language. Nabokov said that people "think not in words but in shadows of words." He fills *Lolita* with satiric caricatures, subverted conversational banalities, and constantly shifting tones.

Characters in *Lolita*

Aunt Sybil: Humbert's maternal aunt. After Humbert's mother is killed by lightning while picnicking, Aunt Sybil moves in and becomes Humbert's governess and his father's housekeeper. Humbert later hears that Sybil was in love with his father. Aunt Sybil, a superstitious woman, correctly predicted that she would die soon after Humbert's sixteenth birthday.

Barbara Burke: Lolita's friend at Camp Q. Barbara and Lolita take turns having sex with thirteen-year-old Charlie Holmes.

John and Jean Farlow: Charlotte Haze's neighbors. After Charlotte is killed, the Farlows attempt to console Humbert. After Jean dies of cancer, John writes Humbert a wild, rambling letter, explaining that he has married a woman from South America and demanding that Humbert "produce" Lolita.

Gaston Godin: A professor of French at Beardsley College, and a possible double for Humbert—or, more accurately, a fun-house mirror reflection of Humbert. Whereas Humbert is meticulously neat, Godin is slovenly; Humbert is slim and manly, Godin obese; while Humbert dotes on little girls, Godin admires young boys. Godin is described as living a "Beardsley existence." (Aubrey Beardsley was the darling of the sophisticated, decadent *fin-de-siècle* Art Nouveau movement; see page 28.)

Harold Haze: Charlotte's first husband, and Lolita's father. Charlotte tells Humbert about Harold's quirky sexual habits, which amuses Humbert. Charlotte and Harold had a lovely child, a blond boy who died as a baby.

Charlie Holmes: The thirteen-year-old son of Camp Q's headmistress. Charlie seduces both Barbara and Lolita when Lolita is twelve. Lolita is more impressed by Charlie's collection of used condoms, fished out of Lake Climax, than she is by Charlie himself.

Charlotte Haze Humbert: Lolita's mother and Humbert's second wife. Charlotte accessorizes her conversations with a limited number of French phrases (*cheri, monsieur, adieu*), and her home with a mass-produced print of a van Gogh landscape. She is swept away by Humbert's authentic European background, accent, expensive wardrobe, polished manners, and cultured taste in food and perfumes. Charlotte proposes to Humbert, and their brief, less-than-blissful marriage ends when she is struck by a car and killed.

Vladimir Nabokov

Humbert Humbert: The narrator of the story. Plagued by a painful obsession for young girls, Humbert first marries a blonde woman who looks girlish until she removes her makeup. Humbert flees to the United States, where he falls in love with Lolita Haze. She leaves him for Clare Quilty. He writes his memoir from jail, awaiting his trial for Quilty's murder.

Annabel Leigh: A young girl whom Humbert meets at a seaside resort in France. Annabel and Humbert, both teenagers at the time, immediately fall in love. On their last day together, they attempt to explore each other's bodies in a secret cove, but two bearded men interrupt them. An earlier attempt at sexual intimacy was interrupted by Annabel's mother. Four months after the incident in the cave, Annabel dies of typhus.

Louise: Charlotte's black maid. Before Charlotte drives Lolita to Camp Q for the summer, she hands Louise a letter to give to Humbert, confessing her everlasting love for him and proposing to him. After Charlotte marries Humbert, she thinks that the two of them need a full-time, live-in servant who is more cosmopolitan than Louise.

Mr. McCoo: The man who was supposed to host Humbert in Ramsdale but could not because his house burned down. Mr. McCoo has a twelve-year-old daughter, and Humbert is agonized that he lost his chance to ogle the young McCoo girl.

Clare Quilty: A heavy-drinking playwright. Like Humbert, Quilty lusts for young girls, and he attempts to charm Lolita out of Humbert's arms. In conspiracy with Lolita, he shadows Humbert and Lolita, making Humbert paranoid. Eventually, Lolita abandons Humbert and goes with Quilty.

Ivor Quilty: Clare's uncle. Ivor is an overweight Ramsdale dentist who treats Charlotte Haze.

John Ray, Jr.: The editor of Humbert's confession and author of the foreword to it. Ray assures readers that they should have no anxieties about suddenly encountering pornography, for the book contains none. Though Ray admires Humbert the writer, he does not admire Humbert the man, and sees the manuscript as an opportunity to continue waging war against anyone who would prey upon innocent, unsuspecting young girls.

Dolores (Lolita) Haze Schiller: To 37-year-old Humbert, Lolita is both the embodiment of the ideal nymphet and an in-the-flesh reincarnation of his beloved childhood sweetheart, Annabel Leigh. Like most nymphets, Lolita is not only lovely, she possesses an intuitive knowledge of her power to inflame older men's curiosities and libidos. When she and Humbert make love for the first time, he is so apprehensive and fumbling that she calmly takes matters into her own hands. In the end, tired of Humbert's harsh rules, Lolita escapes from him with another older man, Clare Quilty.

Richard (Dick) Schiller: The man Lolita marries after escaping from Quilty's guest ranch. Dick is a war veteran with bad hearing in one ear, and has, as Humbert notes, "[a]rctic blue eyes, black hair, ruddy cheeks, [and an] unshaven chin."

Rita: The woman with whom Humbert lives after Lolita leaves him.

Valeria: Humbert's first wife. Humbert marries Valeria for two reasons: first, because of her skillful makeup, she looks like a little girl; second, Humbert hopes that marriage to Valeria will cure him of his obsession with little girls. Both hopes are dashed immediately. When Valeria removes her makeup and clothes, she becomes a toad-like, big-breasted woman. Humbert becomes more addicted than ever to his search for pale waifs with thin arms and luminous eyes. When Valeria admits that she has fallen in love with a taxi driver, Humbert is delighted to be rid of her.

Reading *Lolita*

Foreword

In his fictional foreword to *Lolita*, Nabokov's character **John Ray, Jr.** begins with facts: **Humbert Humbert**, the author of this work, died in prison of a heart attack on November 16, 1952, just before his trial was scheduled to begin. Humbert's lawyer has asked Ray to edit a memoir that Humbert left behind. Aside from correcting grammatical mistakes and giving real people and places fictional names, Ray has left Humbert's memoir wholly intact. Ray notes that "Humbert" is not the author's real name, and Lolita's fictional last name only rhymes with her real last name. For readers who are curious about the sordid particulars of Humbert's criminal degeneracy, Ray cites the date of the crime, which can easily be researched in newspaper files.

Not a single obscene term can be found in this work, Ray says. He followed the lead of Judge John M. Woolsey and included scenes that are crucial to the story, even though they might *seem* pornographic. Ray marvels that we can love Humbert's lyrical prose while abhorring Humbert's behavior. He hopes that this book will remind parents, teachers, and social workers to be ever vigilant in protecting their innocent children from such depraved monsters as Humbert.

THE HONORABLE
JOHN M. WOOLSEY

James Joyce's *Ulysses* was published in complete form in Paris in 1922, but because a number of critics deemed it pornographic, U.S. Customs and postal officials seized copies of the book when tourists attempted to bring it into the country or mail it to friends. A successful smuggle was the ultimate dare for many fans of literature. Many protesters cried censorship, and in 1933, the year the Prohibition of alcohol was repealed in the U. S., Judge John M. Woolsey overturned the ban on *Ulysses*. Bennett Cerf of Random House immediately set his printers to churning out copies. In his legal decision, Judge Woolsey noted that he had read *Ulysses* in its entirety, including the passages said to be pornographic, and nowhere did he detect the "leer of the sensualist." He added that the so-called objectionable language consisted of common, Old Saxon words, that Joyce was writing honestly about sex, and that his "locale was Celtic, and his season was Spring." The book, therefore, was not pornographic. So compelling and important is Judge Woolsey's decision that it prefaces most editions of *Ulysses*.

PART ONE
Chapters 1–10

Humbert begins his memoir by reflecting on the lovely Lolita, thinking of his various endearments for her: Lo, Lola, Dolly, Dolores—and **Lolita**. He is still infatuated with his memory of the nymphet he loved for less than three years.

Yet she was not the first love of his life. Humbert confesses that before Lolita, there was another "girl-child," as he puts it.

Humbert tells us about himself. He was born in 1910 in Paris. His father was a French-Austrian citizen of Switzerland, and his mother was English. She died in a freak accident involving a picnic and lightning when Humbert was three years old. Humbert was raised by his father and his blue-eyed, poetic **Aunt Sybil**, who correctly predicted that that she would die soon after Humbert turned sixteen. For the most part, Humbert's childhood was happy and sunny, filled with dogs, orange trees, and sandy beaches. His father taught him to

> "As far as I can recall, the initial shiver of inspiration was somehow prompted by a newspaper story about an ape in the Jardin des Plantes who, after months of coaxing by a scientist, produced the first drawing ever charcoaled by an animal: this sketch showed the bars of the poor creature's cage."
>
> **NABOKOV**, "ON A BOOK ENTITLED LOLITA"

swim, dive, and water-ski, and he read *Don Quixote* and *Les Misérables* to him. Rich, cosmopolitan family friends spoiled Humbert with expensive chocolates and adoration. Yet nothing especially memorable happened to Humbert until the summer before he was sent away to private boarding school.

That summer at the beach, he met a girl named **Annabel Leigh**, who was not quite thirteen. On their last day together, Humbert and Annabel found a cave and began to kiss and explore each other's bodies. A pair of bearded gentlemen interrupted them.

On an earlier night, in a mimosa grove behind Annabel's villa, the two had kissed and Humbert had put "the scepter of [his] passion" in Annabel's fist. As Humbert writes, he can recall Annabel's smell of biscuits, her perfume. The sound of her mother's voice interrupted them. Four months later, Annabel died of typhus. Annabel left behind a lonely ache that remained in Humbert's veins until years later, when Lolita broke Annabel's enchantment.

As a college-age man, Humbert initially planned to study psychiatry, but instead studied literature in Paris and London, published a few academic papers, and began compiling a manual of French literature for English-speaking students. For a while, he taught school and did social work in orphanages and reform schools, where he was able to gaze at prepubescent girl-children. Few of them kindled his interest, however. Slowly he began to formulate his theory of the nymphet: a demon girl-child between nine and fourteen who may or may not recognize her power to ignite passion in much older men. Annabel, he says, was lovely, but not a nymphet to him at the time, because Humbert himself was a young man, a "faunlet."

Psychological theories of sexuality frightened Humbert, and he comforted himself with the knowledge that the Italian poets Dante (1265–1321) and Petrarch (1303–1374) were both obsessed with girl-children.

Finally, thinking that marriage might cure his obsession with nymphets, Humbert married a blonde woman, the "fluffy" **Valeria.** Humbert liked Valeria because she looked like a child, but she soon became a yoke around his neck. Fate smiled on Humbert when he inherited several thousand dollars, contingent on a move to the United States and a demonstration of interest in his American uncle's perfume business. Almost simultaneously, Valeria declared her love for another man, a taxi driver.

Humbert mentions that the prison's library includes a book called *Who's Who in the Limelight*. One entry in the *Who's Who* is for **Clare Quilty**, playwright and author of *The Little Nymph.* Quilty's plays also include *The Woman Who Loved Lightning, The Strange Mushroom*, and *Fatherly Love*. The *Who's Who* entry mentions Quilty's love of fast cars and includes statistics about his plays on tour and his performances "on the road."

Suddenly single, Humbert works in New York, suffers a series of nervous breakdowns, and is encouraged to quiet his anxieties in a small-town atmosphere.

Humbert goes to the New England village of Ramsdale, prepared to live with a **Mr. McCoo** and his wife, baby, and twelve-year-old daughter. When no one meets him at the train station, Humbert checks into the town's only hotel, where Mr. McCoo finds him and informs him that the McCoos' house has burned down. The McCoos have "fled to a farm," and arrangements have been made for Humbert to rent a room from **Mrs. Charlotte Haze**. On his way to Mrs. Haze's house, Humbert is horrified by the banality of Ramsdale and makes plans to leave as soon as he has graciously declined Mrs. Haze's offer of hospitality. His driver suddenly swerves to avoid a dog.

A black maid, **Louise**, answers the doorbell of the Haze residence and leaves Humbert to wait in the foyer, face-to-face with a Mexican icon and a print of an all-too-familiar van Gogh landscape. Mrs. Haze comes downstairs. She has plucked eyebrows and a brown bun and wears maroon slacks. She shows Humbert the messy house and the backyard where, in a pool of sunlight, a nymphet resembling Annabel sits half-naked. This girl looks at Humbert over her sunglasses, and blinks her eyes. Mrs. Haze says that the child is "my Lo" and calls Humbert's attention to her lilies. "Beautiful," he says, "beautiful, beautiful."

UNDERSTANDING AND INTERPRETING
Part One, Chapters 1–10

A Crafty Preface: Nabokov includes a preface to the novel in the form of a foreword written by a fictional editor, Ray. This foreword enhances the illusion that we are about to read a real confession, and it answers in advance the critics who, Nabokov knows, will call *Lolita* perverted and pornographic. Jay says he merely corrected grammatical errors, leaving intact unsavory passages—a decision supported by the legal precedent set by Judge Woolsey—because leaving them out would bleed the story of its pathos. By referring to Woolsey, Nabokov implies that *Lolita* should be compared to *Ulysses*, an acknowledged masterpiece that was reviled by critics and called pornographic when it was first published. Ray also calls Humbert's confession a warning, saying it should remind us to watch over our children.

An Unmentioned Crime: Nabokov structures his novel as a long confession written for the "ladies and gentlemen of the jury." He asks his readers to be his ultimate judge and jury, for these "notes"—this novel—will not be used in his legal defense, nor will they be published until Lolita is dead. Thus, regardless of the sentence handed down by the legal authorities, Humbert is most concerned with how we, his readers, judge him. Only we will know the full story, the truth, about him and Lolita and the crime he committed. But to what crime is he referring? As yet, we don't know, although we might guess that he is referring to child molestation or statutory rape. Humbert wants to defend himself, for it is clear that he thinks himself an innocent man. He refers to his confession as a "tangle of thorns," an allusion to the tangle of thorns placed on Christ's head prior to his crucifixion. With this allusion, Humbert likens himself to Christ, implying that like Christ he is unjustly persecuted.

POE'S NYMPHET BLUEPRINT

Nabokov became fond of Edgar Allan Poe's (1809–1849) poetry when he was a child and continued reading Poe as an adult. Like Poe, Nabokov was interested in the bizarre and the macabre, qualities visible in *Lolita*. Humbert's overwhelming obsession with Lolita is pathologically bizarre. Clare Quilty's jaded fascination with young girls, pornography, and drugs is macabre, as is Humbert's fixation on doing violence to Quilty. Nabokov was especially fond of Poe's poem "Annabel Lee," about a maiden who lives by the sea. In the poem, the narrator remembers being a child with Annabel Lee. He says he will dream of her forever even though she has been taken away from him. Nabokov's character Annabel Leigh is likely an homage to Poe's Annabel Lee. Besides the almost identical names, Nabokov's Annabel Leigh lives by the sea and exists in Humbert's mind as an eternal child, an object of permanent devotion, just like the young girl in Poe's poem.

Meaningful Frivolity: The Mexican icon Humbert encounters in the Haze house symbolizes Humbert himself. During the late 1940s and early 1950s, long dowel-and-yarn Mexican creations called *ojos de Dios* were popular in middle-class American homes, along with hammered-tin Mexican mirror frames, serapes draped over the back of couches, and mass-produced rustic figurines in the shape of fattened quails. The *ojos de Dios* were made of yarn woven around crossbars to make a diamond-shaped pattern. These *ojos de Dios* were rumored to be real Evil Eyes.

Humbert is like this yarn trinket, both pleasant and possibly evil. Throughout the novel, he professes to be a kindly, godly man anxiously looking after the welfare of his stepchild, but he is also the man who eyes Lolita lasciviously, concocting underhanded plots to seduce her.

Return of the Sunglasses: Humbert instantly falls for Lolita, who seems to be an exact physical replica of Annabel, the girl Humbert so loved as a teenager. Nabokov underlines Lolita's connection to Annabel by including a pair of sunglasses in the scene. When young Humbert attempted to make love to Annabel, the only witness was a lost pair of sunglasses. When Humbert sees Lolita for the first time, she is blinking at him over a pair of dark sunglasses, an accessory that links her to Annabel.

Doubles: Nabokov exults in word games and doubles. In *Lolita*, the hero's name is Humbert Humbert, the lawyer's name is Clarence Choate Clark, and Lolita's name, with its two l's, is alliterative. Annabel and Lolita are doubles; both girls obsess Humbert when they are preteens. Furthermore, both Annabel and Humbert have mixed parentage. The novel itself had two titles in manuscript form: *Lolita, or the Confession of a White Widowed Male*. This double title is an important way to understand the novel. *Lolita* is not really about Lolita, it is about Humbert. Only now and then does Humbert try to imagine Lolita's feelings and reactions. He describes Lolita only through the prism of his own perceptions. *Lolita* is Humbert's confession and an exploration of his own psyche.

Prelude and Overture: *Lolita* can be interpreted as a long mood symphony. The first chapters are merry and lively, buoyant with good spirits. In the beginning of his confession, Humbert charms us with his dazzling use of the English language. He is a magician, an entertainer, and a performer. When Humbert speaks of his childhood and youth, his tone is exuberant. He lost his mother when he was a child, but he describes the loss with stoicism and philosophical breeziness. She died quickly, struck dead while on a merry outing, and Humbert thinks that the only thing to do is get on with life. Humbert manages to make the most upsetting situations amusing. His memories of Lolita are heady and playful, and he shows us the exhilaration of being free of his empty-headed wife, Valeria. His nervous collapse fails to depress him, and America's commercial insipidness does not daunt him. In fact, the blandness of the suburbs fires his sense of the satiric. The first section marks the novel's frothiest, highest spirits. From here on, chapter by chapter, the mood becomes darker.

PART ONE

Chapters 11–22

Speaking abruptly to his readers, Humbert cites a pocket diary that he kept during his stay at the Hazes' house. This chapter consists entirely of entries from the diary. In one entry, Humbert writes that merely seeing Lolita's tanned, sun-dappled arms removing clothes from a clothesline "plucked at the most secret and sensitive chord" of his body. Charlotte always interrupts Humbert's reveries, snapping photographs of "Hum" and "Lo." Humbert thinks it a terrible waste that Lolita's great nymphet beauty will disappear untasted with puberty. Even worse will be her eventual metamorphosis into a clone of her "mamma."

Humbert confesses that it is madness to keep a journal, but his handwriting is miniscule and only a "loving wife" would take the time to try to read it. Although Humbert realizes that Lolita is imperfect, he is nevertheless smitten, and she seems to encourage him. When Lolita has something in her eye, she agrees to let Humbert get out the speck with his tongue. On a different day, as Humbert writes in his diary, Lolita comes into his room and slides onto his knee.

Humbert tries on a new pair of swimming trunks, anticipating an outing to Hourglass Lake. Once again, "the mamma" intrudes and asks him to go shopping. Lolita dashes for the car and squeezes next to Humbert. Secretly, she slips her hand into his, and Humbert strokes it all the way to the department store. At home again, Lolita steals up behind Humbert and claps her hands over his eyes.

> "For Virtue in her daily Race,
>   Like Janus bears a double Face;
>   Looks back with Joy where she has gone,
> And therefore goes with Courage on."
>
> **JONATHAN SWIFT**

One afternoon while Charlotte is at church, Humbert attempts to wrestle a magazine from Lolita. She feigns resistance, then collapses with her legs across his lap. Humbert begins talking while gently rolling his thighs against her legs until he achieves sexual climax underneath his pajamas and robe. Almost simultaneously, Lolita runs to answer the ringing telephone.

That night, over a candlelight dinner, Charlotte tells Humbert that Lolita will be going to a summer camp for young girls. Annoyed, Humbert feigns an excruciating toothache. Charlotte suggests that he telephone **Ivor Quilty**, her dentist. Humbert goes to his room.

From his window, Humbert watches Charlotte and Lolita leave for camp. Lolita impulsively dashes upstairs and kisses Humbert before leaving.

Louise comes in and gives Humbert a letter from Charlotte. In it, Charlotte declares her passionate love for "mon cher, cher monsieur" and pleads with him to leave now, for if he is there when she returns, she will take it as proof that he loves her and will marry her.

Humbert lies in Lolita's bed. He dreads Charlotte and wants to leave, but if he stays, he will become Lolita's stepfather, a happy outcome. Humbert decides he can endure Charlotte's bad taste, bad food, and bad French. He celebrates his decision to stay by drinking several glasses of gin and pineapple juice. He fantasizes about drugging both mother and daughter so that he can consummate his passion for Lolita.

Charlotte and Humbert are married quickly and quietly. Charlotte vows to love Humbert always, but swears she will commit suicide if she ever discovers that Humbert does not believe in her Christian god. Charlotte redecorates the house and orders a new double bed. When Humbert has sex with Charlotte, he imagines that her body was once as lovely as Lolita's. Charlotte and Humbert begin socializing with **Jean and John Farlow**.

In private, Charlotte nightly asks Humbert to tell her of his old sexual trysts in Europe, and he obliges her by making up stories. Charlotte tells him about her blond son, who died long ago. Charlotte hopes that she and Humbert can conceive a child together. She impulsively rails against Lolita. Away at camp, Lolita scrawls postcards to "Mummy and Hummy."

One morning at Hourglass Lake, Charlotte says she wants to hire a full-time, "real trained servant maid" and send Lolita straight from camp to a good boarding school. Disturbed, Humbert begins to imagine murdering Charlotte. Humbert looks around as they swim. No one can see them. He realizes that if he were to dive down, seize Charlotte's ankles, and drown her, no one would know. He confesses that he just could not do it. He and his trusting mate go back to their towels. Moments later, Jean Farlow, who is an artist, comes toward them and says that she saw them while painting the lake.

EROTIC ART NOUVEAU

Widely acknowledged as the foremost illustrator of the Art Nouveau movement (1890–1914) in Europe and the United States, Aubrey Beardsley (1872–1898) produced highly stylized, erotic, often perverse drawings of male and female nudes. His female nudes were usually high-breasted, bold temptresses, and his male nudes sported enormous erections. Not surprisingly, Beardsley's illustrations often overpowered the text they were designed to accompany. Beardsley was a satirist, like Nabokov. The men were similarly interested in mocking closeted middle-class sex fantasies and playing on anxieties, repressions, and men's fears of female superiority. Nabokov offends middle-class sensibilities by imagining twelve-year-old Lolita as a siren who lures men to their deaths. He acknowledges his kinship with Beardsley in *Lolita*, naming a town, Beardsley, after the artist, and referring to fate as Aubrey McFate.

Charlotte announces that in the fall, the two of them are going to England. Humbert erupts, saying he refuses to go and is sick of Charlotte showing him off. He rails on as Charlotte, devastated, falls to her knees and crawls to him, swearing that he is her ruler and god. Humbert says he means to spend a good deal of time alone in his room, writing.

After that, Charlotte rarely intrudes on Humbert's privacy. One day, however, she comes in and asks Humbert if the little drawer in the bedside table is always locked. Humbert jokes that it contains locked-up love letters. Charlotte sarcastically asks if "his lordship" might enjoy spending the fall in New England, at a hotel called The Enchanted Hunters. After she leaves, Humbert checks to make sure the key to the locked desk drawer is still hidden.

Humbert has been experimenting by using prescription drugs, which he obtains on the pretext of nerves and sleeplessness, to drug Charlotte. He asks his doctor for the strongest pill that can be prescribed, and the doctor gives him a sample vial of new pills. Coming home, Humbert sees Charlotte, distraught and writing a letter at her bureau. She says wrathfully, "The Haze woman, the big bitch, the old cat, the obnoxious mamma," repeating the words Humbert used in his diary to refer to her. She tells him she is leaving tonight and he will never see "that miserable brat again." In his room, Humbert sees a key dangling from the locked drawer where he keeps his diary. He grabs a bottle of Scotch, thinking that liquor will soothe Charlotte's rage. He tells Charlotte that she is crazy—what she read were fragments of a novel. Charlotte continues writing. Humbert makes Charlotte a drink and calls to her that it is ready. She does not answer. "Mad bitch," he thinks to himself. The phone rings; a neighbor has called to tell Humbert that Charlotte has been run over by a car.

UNDERSTANDING AND INTERPRETING
Part One, Chapters 11–22

Humbert Indulges Himself: While *Lolita* includes several erotic scenes, it never describes the details of physical coupling, a vagueness that suits Humbert's conception of himself. For Humbert, sex with Lolita exists as an ideal. His quest to sleep with her seems like an impossible dream, not a realistic project to be imagined in gritty detail. Humbert indulges himself in fantasies and forgives himself for them, describing his own attraction to Lolita with stylistic care. He is convinced that he is not a lecher hell-bent on raping Lolita, but a poet with an overactive libido. Appropriately, then, he skims over his sexual fantasies without providing the unseemly details that would make him unsavory in his readers' eyes.

Dreaming of Death: Violent undercurrents seethe beneath Humbert's charming, lyric prose. He imagines various scenarios of death for "the mamma," "the old cat," Charlotte Haze. Charlotte is Humbert's rival and roadblock. She interrupts his erotic dreaming of Lolita, and despite her crankiness, she wants to protect her daughter and make her stop behaving badly. Charlotte's understandable instincts enrage Humbert, and he yearns for some wonderful natural disaster to kill Charlotte. Not only does Humbert imagine natural death, he contemplates murdering the pesky Charlotte. As he swims with her in Hourglass Lake, he is tempted to dive down, grab her ankles, and drown her.

Mother versus Daughter: Charlotte and Lolita compete against each another for Humbert's attention as if they are unrelated rivals, equal in age. Charlotte is determined that Humbert will be her husband, and Lolita is experimenting with her emerging sexuality, testing her caregivers to see how far she can go. Lolita may not know the extent of her effect on Humbert, but she understands, for example, that resting her legs on Humbert's thighs is a provocation. She knows that she has the power to unnerve Humbert and madden her mother, as she proves when she makes a wild dash for the car and hurls herself inside, sitting next to Humbert and letting him hold her hand. Charlotte is not explicitly aware that Humbert lusts after her daughter. She thinks Lolita is a pest, making a nuisance of herself and flirting with Humbert to annoy her mother.

Dear Diary: Nabokov breaks up Humbert's first-person narration with the inclusion of journal entries, letters, and postcards, all of which heighten the illusion that Humbert's is a true story. Humbert inserts a long series of journal entries written during his first days at Ramsdale. The journal primarily details his distaste for Charlotte, her bland cooking, her fraudulent air of sophistication, and her maddening imposition of herself between him and Lolita. By including the journal entries, Humbert offers us his most private, honest thoughts. Nabokov also includes in his novel the text of Lolita's postcard to "Mummy and Hummy," and Charlotte's letter of proposal to Humbert, both documents that heighten our sense that we are reading a true chronicle.

Satirizing the Suburbs: Charlotte's letter of proposal to Humbert gives Nabokov an opportunity to satirize suburban pretensions. In her letter, Charlotte displays all of the qualities that repulse Humbert—her fervor for God, her melodramatic use of French, her banal American slang, her abusive references to Lolita, and her ignorance of the inner life of the man she seeks to catch. One of the juiciest bits of irony in Charlotte's letter is her insistence that, if Humbert were to use his knowledge of her love for him to seduce her, he would be a "criminal—worse than a kidnapper who rapes a child." In her melodramatic hyperbole, Charlotte unknowingly hits the bull's eye.

Small Dogs and Comic Irony: In *Lolita*, many incidences of comic irony stem from actions that initially seem unimportant and later prove to be of major significance. In Chapter 22, comic irony centers around a little dog. The driver who brought Humbert to the Haze house had to swerve sharply in order to avoid killing the dog, an incident that seemed meaningless at the time. Now we see that it was a foreshadowing of Charlotte's doom, for she is killed when a car swerves sharply to avoid hit-

> " It [*Lolita*] is also, not to change the subject, just about the funniest book I remember having read."
>
> **JOHN HOLLANDER**, *NEW YORK REVIEW OF BOOKS*

ting a little dog and hits her. Humbert, who has been wishing for a calamity to take Charlotte's life, gets his wish when Charlotte is hit and killed. Suddenly, no one is watching over Lolita, and he is free to do whatever he wishes with her.

PART ONE
Chapters 23–33

Humbert runs outside and sees a big black Packard automobile on a neighbor's lawn. Neighbors and policemen are on the scene. Charlotte's corpse lies underneath a tartan robe. She was hit as she ran toward the mailbox with three letters. A child hands the letters to Humbert, who immediately stuffs them into his pockets and begins shredding them with his fingers.

John and Jean Farlow take Humbert upstairs and tuck him into Lolita's bed. The Farlows stay in the master bedroom for the night. The next day, Humbert confides to the Farlows that he and Charlotte had a love affair long ago, when he was married and she was engaged to **Harold Haze**. As Humbert hoped, Jean assumes that Humbert must be Lolita's biological father.

Humbert makes plans to fetch Lolita. He wonders if Lolita has somehow learned of Charlotte's death, and if he should legally adopt her. As a black thundercloud hovers over Ramsdale, Humbert takes Charlotte's little blue sedan onto the highway. He decides to tell Lolita that Charlotte is ill and about to undergo major surgery. Then, he will take Lolita from hotel to hotel, on their way toward the non-existent hospital, until a time when he will pretend her mother has died.

Vladimir Nabokov

From a nearby town, Humbert phones the camp and tells the camp mistress that Lolita's mother is gravely ill and he will arrive tomorrow to pick up Lolita. On the way to camp, Humbert stops and buys Lolita all manner of clothes, including pajamas. Realizing that her summer camp is not far from The Enchanted Hunters, he calls and reserves a room with twin beds. Then he silently exults over his forty violet sleeping pills.

Arriving at camp next day, Humbert is reading about Lolita's mediocre behavior as a camper when she comes in dragging a heavy suitcase. She is taller and thinner than she was when she left. In the car, she asks how her mother is. Humbert says that the trouble seems to be abdominal. Lolita grunts single-syllable responses to Humbert's questions and sneeringly refers to him as "Dad." She soon softens, though, and asks how he fell in love with her mother. Humbert speaks of spiritual relationships, saying Lolita knows nothing about such things. She scoffs at this, saying she has been "revoltingly unfaithful" to him—which is just as well since he no longer cares for her.

Humbert stops the car and Lolita kisses him with peppermint breath only moments before a policeman pulls up beside them to ask if they've seen a blue sedan the same make as theirs. After the cop leaves, Lolita asks Humbert if he thinks Charlotte would be furious to know that the two of them are lovers. She talks about camp and washing dishes there. Humbert kisses the back of her neck, and she snaps at him, saying she does not want a dirty old man drooling on her.

Lolita is awed by the vastness of The Enchanted Hunters. At the front desk, Humbert discovers that the room he reserved has already been rented, and he and Lolita will have to share a double bed. Lolita says her mother will divorce him and strangle her when she finds out about this escapade. Humbert objects, saying sometimes it is necessary when traveling for father and daughter to sleep together. Lolita says, "The word is incest."

At dinner, Lolita seems to recognize a fellow diner as Mr. Quilty, a Hollywood writer whose picture appeared in a Dromes cigarette ad. Humbert displays his sleeping pills, knowing that Lolita will be curious. They are Vitamin X pills, he explains, and as he hoped, she begs for one. He pretends to swallow one, and Lolita swallows hers immediately. She seems so sleepy that Humbert takes her to their room and tells her to undress and go to bed. He says he is going back to the lobby and will return later.

Humbert strolls out onto the porch of the hotel, waiting for the pill to take its effect. He hears a voice in the darkness ask him where he got the girl. The narration is ambiguous here, leaving open the possibility that Humbert mishears the stranger. Humbert answers curtly that she is his daughter and explains that the girl's mother is dead. The stranger in the darkness is not convinced that the girl is Humbert's daughter. He invites the two of them to have lunch with him tomorrow. Humbert declines, saying they are leaving early.

Back in the room, Lolita is asleep. She wakes momentarily and calls Humbert "**Barbara**." Humbert realizes that the purple pill is not working. He slips in beside Lolita and tries to touch her shoulder, but she bolts upright and begins tossing. Humbert lies awake for most of the night, occasionally lulled by "a breeze from wonderland." By six o'clock the next morning, Lolita is wide awake. Humbert abruptly tells us that by quarter past the hour, they have had sex. And, he claims, it was Lolita who seduced him.

While eating potato chips, a mealy banana, and bruised peaches, Lolita explains that her first lover was **Charlie Holmes**, the son of the camp mistress, who also had sex with her friend Barbara. Charlie was not particularly sexy, but he had an impressive collection of used contraceptives that he had fished out of Lake Climax.

While Humbert checks out of the hotel, Lolita reads a movie magazine. A man in tweeds, about Humbert's age, ogles her. On the road, Lolita teases Humbert, saying she should tell the police how Humbert raped her, and calling him a "dirty old man." Confused and worried that he physically hurt her by mistake, Humbert stops at a gas station. Lolita wants to call her mother. Humbert tells her that her mother is dead.

At the next hotel, Humbert asks for separate rooms, but in the middle of the night, Lolita creeps into his bed, sobbing. Lolita, Humbert observes, has "nowhere else to go."

> "My private tragedy… is that I had to abandon my natural idiom, my untrammeled, rich, and infinitely docile Russian tongue for a second-rate brand of English, devoid of any of those apparatuses—the baffling mirror, the black velvet backdrop, the implied associations and traditions—which the native illusionist, frac-tails flying, can magically use to transcend the heritage his own way."
>
> **NABOKOV**, "ON A BOOK ENTITLED LOLITA"

A WIND FROM WONDERLAND

Humbert makes reference to Wonderland, a creation of Lewis Carroll (Charles L. Dodgson (1832–1898)). Wonderland is the setting for a novel that Carroll wrote for his favorite prepubescent, nymphet friend, the large-eyed Alice Liddell. Dodgson often photographed Liddell and her sisters in poses that have been interpreted as provocative, occasionally disheveled or half-clad,

 although there is no evidence that he had sexual relationships with them. He doted on Alice and wrote *Alice in Wonderland* for her amusement. *Alice in Wonderland* is among the only Victorian books for children that is neither didactic nor dogmatic. Unlike most other children's books, *Alice* did not include a moral at the end of each chapter. Like Dodgson, Humbert is enamored of young girls. Wonderland affords him a little sleep, a connection that suggests Humbert's affinity with Carroll.

UNDERSTANDING AND INTERPRETING
Part One, Chapters 23–33

The Role of Chance: Nabokov makes chance so great a player in this novel, it is almost as if he is inviting us to laugh with him at his authorly interference. By chance, Humbert's disappointing first wife runs off with another man, relieving the bored Humbert. By chance, Humbert comes to Ramsdale, where he discovers the perfect nymphet, Lolita, almost a reincarnation of his beloved Annabel. By chance, Charlotte dies, neatly fulfilling Humbert's dreams of fate (Aubrey McFate, as he calls it; see page 28) striking down Charlotte. Charlotte dies on her way to mail three letters that could ruin Humbert's reputation and spoil his plans for Lolita, but by chance, a child innocently hands Humbert the letters that were flung from Charlotte's hand.

Uncomfortable Irony: Nabokov makes us squirm with his ironies. It is a child that hands Humbert a reprieve by giving him the letters, and therefore it is a child that inadvertently delivers a fellow child, Lolita, into the hands of a molester. In another uncomfortable irony, the Farlows, loving and concerned neighbors, tuck the stunned Humbert not into Charlotte's bed, but into Lolita's bed.

Dramatic Irony: Dramatic irony results when we, the readers, know something that one of the main characters in a novel does not know. For example, dramatic irony results when the Farlows attempt to comfort Humbert and he spins outlandish, romantic tales, saying it is tragic that Charlotte was killed just after they had been reunited. He lies, saying that he and Charlotte were lovers long ago. We know that Humbert's story is an abominable falsehood from beginning to end, but Jean Farlow does not. She concludes that Humbert impregnated Charlotte during their brief affair, and that Humbert is thus Lolita's real father.

Humbert on the Road: From Chapter 24 on, Humbert spends most of his time on the road, driving, sometimes aimlessly, sometimes according to Lolita's whims, and sometimes with deadly purpose. He always drives Charlotte's small sedan. Humbert believes himself superior to America, but he must travel its roads in a humble, nondescript car.

Delaying Gratification: Humbert could have driven to Camp Q and picked up Lolita the day after Charlotte's death, but he decides to wait and heighten his anticipation. His decision to step back from the culmination of his plan for seduction allows Humbert to preen and comment on his "boyishly manly" behavior. This period of waiting, besides allowing Humbert time to lick his chops, also allows doubts and fears to creep into his consciousness. He wonders if, somehow, Lolita will have learned of Charlotte's death. He wonders if he should adopt her. Arriving at the camp, he is reassured that she knows nothing, and he delays still further, buying fantasy outfits for Lolita.

Hollywood Appeal: In dining room of The Enchanted Hunters, Lolita sees someone who, she says, resembles Quilty. Humbert thinks that Lolita is referring to Charlotte's dentist, who is also named Quilty (and happens to be Clare's uncle) but Lolita is thinking of Clare Quilty, "the writer fellow in the Dromes [cigarette] ad." Lolita is obsessed with Hollywood and celebrities, and Quilty has written for Hollywood.

A Brush with the Law: After Lolita impulsively kisses Humbert and a police car drives up alongside them, Lolita scolds Humbert and sarcastically says it is a wonder he was not arrested. She could have been referring to his plans to have sex with a minor, but she says she was only talking about his terrible driving. He has been exceeding the speed limit, thinking only of having the girl beside him. Humbert's encounter with the police officer foreshadows another encounter later in the novel.

Consummation: Surprisingly, sex happens not because Humbert orchestrates it, but because Lolita does. After Humbert's meticulous preparation to rape Lolita, chance intervenes: the knockout pills, supposedly strong enough to drug a cow, do not work. Lolita is restless and woozy all night long, and Humbert cannot rape her. The faulty pills, perhaps combined with Humbert's nervousness, take agency away from Humbert. Almost comically, Lolita seduces Humbert— at least according to him. Now, halfway through the novel, Humbert and Lolita have had speedy sex, and Humbert's quivering fantasies have became fact. Humbert is not only Lolita's stepfather, he is her lover. A turning point has been reached.

Unreliable Humbert: We have only Humbert's unreliable version of events, and he makes himself suspect by insisting that Lolita instigated sex and then took it in stride. Humbert is convincing in this portrait of himself as passive victim of Lolita's harlotry, and it is only when he occasionally reveals his cruelty— telling Lolita in a curt sentence that her mother is dead, for example, or taking pleasure in the realization that she is now alone in the world but for him—that we remember that Humbert is abusing his position as a powerful adult and a father figure.

PART TWO
Chapters 1–15

Humbert and Lolita spend the next year, from August 1947 to August 1948, driving all over the United States.

Along the way, they stay in every kind of lodging. They inspect lighthouses, natural caves, dinosaur tracks, ghost towns, a gun collection in Oklahoma, cows in Kansas, and grottos in Louisiana. They eat what Lolita wants to eat—sundaes, greasy burgers, and French fries—and they listen to songs about careless love and love in all the wrong places. During late afternoons, they loll on lounge chairs or under patio umbrellas. Lolita reads movie magazines and sees dozens of movies.

During one hot, boring afternoon, Lolita discovers gift shops. After that, every time she sees a sign advertising a souvenir shop, she demands that they stop. The back seat soon fills up with Indian curios, dolls, copper jewelry, and cactus candy. Humbert gives Lolita whatever she wants, but she becomes restless. She mopes and complains. Humbert threatens her with incarceration, saying because she is a minor, she could become a ward of the state, dumped in an institution for juvenile delinquents. He tells her that in Sicily, it is considered natural for a father and daughter to sleep together. Humbert mentions a man who pled guilty to "transporting a nine-year-old-girl across states lines for immoral purposes," a crime under the Mann Act. He thinks this law is ridiculous, and points out that Lolita is thirteen, not nine. He says, "I am your father . . . and I love you."

Humbert begins observing Lolita more carefully, and Lolita begins observing the young men who fill their gas tank. She starts flirting with old men and cocky college students and pleading with Humbert to pick up hitchhikers, soldiers, and Mexicans. Humbert says Lolita's "bi-iliac garland [is] still as brief as a lad's."

Humbert enrolls Lolita in the Beardsley School for Girls. Beardsley College for Women, which is in the same town, has a fine library. Humbert's friend **Gaston Godin** teaches at the French department there, and Humbert hopes to win a position at the university through him.

Gaston Godin rents a house for Lolita and Humbert not far from Lolita's school, where Humbert hopes he can discreetly leer at young nymphets as they walk to class. The fall term begins.

Several times a week, Humbert plays chess with Godin, an aging closeted homosexual who likes little boys and tempts them with chocolates.

Lolita begins charging Humbert money for caresses, kisses, and sex, denying him everything unless he pays up. Humbert complains that "[h]er weekly

AS BRIEF AS A BOY'S

Referring to Lolita's rear end as a brief "garland," Humbert makes reference to British writer A. E. Housman (1859–1936), who wrote odes to adolescent male beauty. Housman's poem "To an Athlete Dying Young" (1896), which mourns the death of a young man in the prime of his life, finds solace in the idea that the boy will never live to see his life's triumphs surpassed. Unlike his peers' names, the athlete's name will not die "before the man." The last line of the poem refers to a metaphorical garland of laurels, the bloom of youth, that is "briefer than a girl's" and will remain, unwithered, in the athlete's hair. Nabokov plays off this line when he says that Lolita, not having yet reached puberty, still has a "garland" of buttocks "as brief as a lad's." Like the narrator of Housman's poem, Humbert sees the appeal of halting life at its peak, before the unyielding passage of time transform faunlets into men and nymphets into women.

allowance, paid to her under condition she fulfill her basic obligations," sky-rocketed during her time at Beardsley. Humbert fears that Lolita plans to amass fifty dollars and use it to run off to Hollywood or New York.

Humbert is called to the office of the dean of the school, who is worried about Lolita—or "Dolly," as she calls her. Dolly, the dean tells Humbert, seems to be "still shuttling between the anal and genital zones of development." Lighting a cigarette, she tells him that Dolly is uninterested in sex. The dean asks Humbert to allow Lolita to take part in school dramatics, particularly in their upcoming production, *The Hunted Enchanters.* The dean observed Dolly during an audition and thought her a "perfect little nymph."

Humbert has been extremely controlling, refusing to allow Lolita to talk to boys on the phone or go on dates, but he now decides to let her host a party for girls and boys her own age. The party is a sad affair. The adolescents mess up the kitchen, play cards, and debate predestination. Afterward, Lolita says she finds the boys "revolting." Humbert rewards this remark with a new tennis racket.

Rehearsals for *The Enchanted Hunters* commence, and Lolita begins spending a good deal of time with a girlfriend who flirts with Humbert as well as boys her age. Lolita becomes increasingly untidy, wearing soiled clothes and not bathing. Her legs and thighs thicken.

After Lolita skips a music lesson, she and Humbert argue loudly. A neighbor calls to complain and Lolita runs out of the house. Humbert follows her and sees her inside a phone booth. She turns, sees him watching her, and hangs up. She says that she was trying to reach him and asks him to buy her a coke. On the way home, she announces that she loathes school, hates the play, and wants to leave. She wants the two of them to go on a long trip again, but this time, she will decide where to go. At home, she asks Humbert to carry her upstairs, saying she feels romantic.

Humbert gets Charlotte's car ready for a journey. He tells the dean that he has had an offer from Hollywood to be a consultant on a film, and that he and Lolita will return to Beardsley as soon as the project is finished. Secretly, he ponders the idea of driving across the Mexican border and taking up residence there, because Mexico has no Mann Act.

Lolita seems excited to leave. Humbert cautions her not to be so rash about tossing away one way of life for something totally unexamined. He reminds her that she gave up Ramsdale for camp and then she left camp for the journey with him, and now she is giving up her play for yet another road trip. He asks her to be a little nicer to him, especially now that they are setting out on a new journey.

Vladimir Nabokov

UNDERSTANDING AND INTERPRETING
Part Two, Chapters 1–15

An Ordinary Couple: Humbert describes his year on the road with Lolita in half-sentences, writing an almost stream-of-consciousness recollection. The style of the desciptions in the long travel sections suggests the speed with which the pair travel, and their sense of aimlessness. They cast off without a home base, and they have no destination. Humbert describes no memorable love scenes. He does not recall any golden intimacies. The trip is a collection of blurred snapshots. During the day, they drive, stop where other tourists stop, bicker, and utter banalities. In the evenings, they routinely have sex, which Humbert does not describe. Lolita grumbles that she is tired of staying in stuffy cabins and "never behaving like ordinary people." Of course Lolita is right to say that they are not behaving like ordinary people—she is a child sleeping with her stepfather, who is in his late thirties. In a grotesque parody of normalcy, however, they are exactly like other ordinary couples, having sex, bickering, and shopping in souvenir stores.

Predator and Prey: In Part One, Humbert is the predator, determined to stalk, corner, and ravish his prey. In Part Two, Humbert begins to lose his control of the situation, and he compensates for his loss by trying to control our perception of him. Humbert begins to feel paranoid, worried that people are out to get him. Sex with Lolita seems more public, less secret. Once, while having sex in the mountains, Humbert and Lolita are interrupted by a mother with two children. This interruption reminds us of Humbert's aborted first sexual experience, when he and Annabel were disturbed by two men with beards. Humbert repeatedly stresses to Lolita that their relationship must be kept secret at all costs. No fool, Lolita realizes that Humbert has started to get nervous, and tries to play on the advantage this gives her. Humbert tries to convince us that Lolita abuses him cruelly; he tries to portray himself as a victim. Confident that we will side with him, he whines that greedy Lolita demands more and more money merely for fulfilling "her basic obligations." Humbert thinks it obvious that the "basic obligations" of a little girl, the chores for which she receives her allowance, should include sex with her stepfather. He calls Lolita's new demands for money "a definite drop in [her] morals." He assumes we will agree that her greediness is far more offensive than his sexual demands. At the same time, however, we can interpret Humbert more sympathetically as prey to his own predatory obsession. His need for Lolita seems beyond his control, and he is genuinely distressed that Lolita does not reciprocate his love.

Humbert's Double: At Beardsley, Humbert meets an old academic friend, Gaston Godin, who can be interpreted as Humbert's double. Like most doubles, Godin reveals something new about the man he mirrors. Humbert's initials are HH; Gaston Godin's are GG. Humbert is a pedophile, fond of young nymphet girls; Gaston Godin is a closet pedophile, particularly fond of young boys. Humbert feeds Lolita candy during their year on the road; Gaston Godin feeds his little boys chocolates. What Godin reveals is the shallowness of Humbert's moral understanding. Humbert is particularly disgusted by Gaston Godin because he caresses young boys despite his obesity and bad hygiene. Humbert presents his own pedophilia as more worthy of our understanding than Godin's, because Humbert dresses smartly and practices good hygiene.

The Dean Misunderstands: Some outsiders notice abnormality in Lolita, but none interpret the abnormality correctly. When Beardsley's dean summons Humbert to her office, he is worried that she wishes to confront him with his misdeeds. However, it turns out that far from discovering Lolita's sexual relationship with Humbert, the dean has discovered in Lolita a worrisome *lack* of interest in sex. Humbert knows, as we do, that Lolita is not curious about sex because she is having sex regularly.

Suspect Behavior: Lolita begins to act suspiciously. She lies to Humbert and sneaks out of the house. She begs to be in the school play and then, unexpectedly, says she hates school and the play and wants Humbert to take her out of school. Without wondering what prompted Lolita's sudden change of heart, Humbert immediately pulls her out of school and takes her on the road. Clearly, Lolita has her own agenda. As far as we know, she is not running away from anything at Beardsley. Furthermore, she is tiring of Humbert, so her sudden desire to run away with him seems odd.

PART TWO
Chapters 16–27

Lolita carefully structures the second trip, planning to stop at the Continental Divide, where she hopes to see Indian ceremonial dances, and at Red Rock, where an actress jumped to her death. The motels seem familiar to Humbert, with their cigarette stench and identical vapid pictures hanging above the beds.

Humbert interrupts his narrative and says that by recalling individual days that once blurred together, he can see a pattern. He says he should have sensed

Vladimir Nabokov

much earlier that all was not well. He chalked up as coincidence certain clues that should have alarmed him. Sometimes, he admits, he thought he was mad or seriously paranoid, but now he knows that Lolita was secretly communicating her whereabouts to someone else. At one gas station, she slipped away, ostensibly to use the rest room, and unexpectedly appeared from across a street, complaining that the rest room was occupied.

> "A love affair should always be a honeymoon. And the only way to make sure of that is to keep changing the man; for the same man can never keep it up."
>
> **GEORGE BERNARD SHAW**

Humbert and Lolita chug through Kansas, where Lolita says she grew up. She decides she does not want to stop near her hometown, an enormous relief for Humbert, who is nervous about running into people she knows. Mornings begin slowly. Lolita often lingers in bed and asks Humbert to fetch her some fresh fruit. One time, he returns from getting bananas to find her dressed, wearing lipstick and a thin T-shirt. She says she just went out for a second. Humbert rips off her shirt and roughly makes her submit to sex, worried that she has been unfaithful to him.

Humbert realizes that he is acting like a madman. While Lolita sleeps, he checks to make sure his pistol is loaded. He lifts a small tumbler of gin and toasts his weapon.

Humbert is jealous of every man they encounter, imaging that everyone is trying either to seduce Lolita or to arrest him. Humbert then realizes that a mysterious man in a red convertible is following them. For a while, he fears the man is a detective. Day after day, the red convertible is visible in Humbert's rearview mirror.

One day, Humbert is paying for gas when he sees Lolita making emphatic gestures to a balding man in an oatmeal-colored coat. Back at the car, he asks Lolita about the man, and she says he seemed lost and wanted a map. Humbert says he thinks they are being followed, possibly by a hired detective, and Lolita says sarcastically, "Ignore him, *Dad*." The convertible matches Humbert's speed, always staying behind him. Humbert darts ahead once and believes that he is free of the red avenger.

Humbert and Lolita see a play at a summer theater festival on the Continental Divide. The cast includes seven lovely pubescent girls veiled in colored gauze. Humbert says that the co-authors of the play, one of whom is Clare Quilty, lifted the idea of the veiled girls from a passage of James Joyce's. After the play, Humbert teases Lolita, saying Quilty was probably a lover of hers in Ramsdale. Lolita says she could never have sex with a fat dentist named Quilty.

Collecting their mail in the town of Wace, Humbert finds a letter addressed to Lolita. He tears it open while Lolita drifts away. The letter is from a friend of Lolita's in Beardsley, who says that her parents plan to send her to school in Paris. When Lolita returns, she tells Humbert that she just saw an old friend from Beardsley and stopped to have a Coke with her. Humbert drills her with questions, and she admits to lying, explaining they simply window-shopped. Back in the car, Humbert finds that Lolita erased the license plate number of the red convertible, which he had written down. Humbert drives out of Wace and slaps Lolita hard. They reconcile and drive back to Wace, where Humbert spots the red convertible again. Later, driving in the Colorado mountains, Humbert is sure that he has trapped his pursuer. At that moment, he gets a flat tire.

Humbert gets out of the car and walks toward the other car. He looks back for a moment and sees his car creeping forward with Lolita at the wheel. He races back and leaps inside. The other car makes a U-turn and disappears.

Playing tennis with Lolita in Colorado, Humbert admires her apricot-colored arms, white shorts, slim waist, and natural gift for the game. He imagines Lolita winning at Wimbledon and turning gratefully toward her graying husband-coach, old Humbert. A bellboy interrupts the daydream, saying that Humbert has a long-distance telephone message. Going inside, Humbert finds there was no long distance phone call at all. He has been the butt of a joke. He asks for a stiff drink at the bar and watches Lolita volley balls with a round-headed man in brown slacks, who slaps her on the buttocks with his racket. Humbert walks toward the tennis court, and the man runs away. Lolita offers no explanation and leaves to change into her swimming suit.

As Lolita plays with a dog, Humbert notices a man watching her with "the same beatitude and grimness" as he sees on her face, though the expression is "made hideous by his maleness."

At the Silver Spur Court in Elphinstone, Lolita complains that she feels terrible. Her head is scalding hot. Humbert takes her to a hospital, hoping that Lolita will not slip into a delirium and begin babbling about their sexual escapades. A few days pass, and Humbert visits Lolita regularly, bringing her armloads of books. Lolita receives a letter in an envelope labeled "Ponderosa Lodge." Lolita tells Humbert to stop using French phrases, since it annoys everyone. She asks him to bring her some of her things.

Humbert returns to their room and starts to pack. He becomes so feverish he cannot leave the motel, so he sends her bags over with someone else. The next day, he learns that Lolita checked herself out of the hospital and the motel and drove away with someone she called her uncle in a black Cadillac.

Vladimir Nabokov

Humbert visits 342 motels, hotels, and tourist homes in his futile search for Lolita, but she is gone. He disposes of her things and then spends several months in a Quebec sanatorium, fearing for his sanity.

In a bar one night, Humbert meets a woman in her thirties named Rita. They become lovers and travel around the country for two years. Humbert tells Rita of his quest to find Lolita and shows her his revolver. She toys with the gun and it explodes, firing a bullet into a water line next door.

Humbert moves in with Rita in New York. One day, he gets two letters. The first is from John Farlow, who says that Jean died and he married a woman from South America. Farlow also says that no one seems to know the whereabouts of little Dolly Haze and Humbert had better "produce her." The other letter is from Lolita, who says that she is married to a man named Richard Schiller, pregnant, and out of money. She and Richard want to move to Alaska, and they need three or four hundred dollars. Lolita begs for a letter from "Dad." She says she has gone through much sadness and hardship and signs the letter "Yours expecting, Dolly."

UNDERSTANDING AND INTERPRETING
Part Two, Chapters 16–27

Across the Great Divide: During the second tour, Lolita wants to visit the Continental Divide, high in the mountains of Colorado. This geographical designation foreshadows the separation—physical, emotional, and geographical—that occurs between Lolita and Humbert when she leaves him and disappears with a mystery man. Humbert is convinced that Lolita and this man have been continually in contact and that she has been slipping out to see him. For a time, when he fears that the man is a detective, Humbert becomes even more paranoid about being followed and imprisoned, as well as about Lolita's possible plans to escape. He knows she has been lying to him about leaving their cabin when he is away on errands. Despite his fears, however, Humbert still worships Lolita. Watching her play tennis, he marvels at her skill and appreciates her sleek curves, silky hair, and smiling radiance as she volleys balls to her opponent.

Pistols and Peckers: An atmosphere of violence builds as Humbert's suspicions mount up. Humbert has a gun and increasingly pats it, checks it, and broods about it. He intends to shoot the man following him and Lolita, and he is experienced with his weapon. Humbert hunted for sport back in Ramsdale and killed, among other things, a woodpecker. The mystery man is like a woodpecker, torturing Humbert by incessantly aggravating his suspicions, fears, and anxieties.

Lolita

The Import of Dogs: Dogs foreshadow increasingly ominous events. Years ago, as Humbert was arriving in Ramsdale, his driver had to swerve to avoid killing a dog. This foreshadowed the deadly incident in which a car swerved to avoid a dog and killed Charlotte. In this section, as Lolita plays with a dog, Humbert sees an ominous man staring at her. Humbert can see that what makes the man's fixed gaze so creepy is his "maleness," but he is unaware that in describing the grotesque, leering man, he has described himself.

Slowly Darkening Tone: *Lolita* begins with sparkling, spirited descriptions of Humbert's past, his first love, Annabel, his education in Europe, his disastrous marriage, and his decision to come to the United States. Those chapters are shot through with sharp wit and verve. Humbert oozes refined, Old World savoir-faire. He describes even tragic incidents with weary good humor. The novel's mood darkens when Humbert realizes that in order to have sex with Lolita, he must remain in Ramsdale and marry Charlotte. Humbert fantasizes about accidental death and murder. "Aubrey McFate" then kills off Charlotte, as easily as he had handed Humbert a divorce from Valeria and granted him a hefty inheritance from a rich American uncle. Ebullience builds once more, climaxing when Humbert successfully spirits Lolita away from Camp Q and into bed. After they have sex, however, the tone of Humbert's narrative becomes strained and tense, and his attempts at humor seem forced.

Humbert feels increasingly that he is no longer in control of his situation. Lolita has the upper hand much of the time. When Humbert realizes that he is being followed by a devious, possibly dangerous stranger, the mood of his confession darkens dramatically. Humbert's vivacious, acerbic wit turns vicious and mean. Lolita leaves and Humbert cannot find her. Her new man has spirited her away, just as Humbert once did. It is as if the smart, self-satisfied spirit that animated the first part of the novel has turned on Humbert and begun mocking him.

Lolita's Letter: Lolita's letter gives us a quick sketch of her adult personality, allowing her to reintroduce herself in her own voice. Humbert can scarcely believe that the letter from Lolita is real, and yet he recognizes her childish scrawl. Reading her letter, which Humbert quotes in full in his confession, we realize that Lolita has changed. She no longer teases or indulges in teenage vernacular. She is Dick Schiller's wife, heavy with child and worried about her lack of finances. Her letter, as a result, cuts to the chase: she wants Humbert to send her money. She does not want her husband to know about her request for charity, but she wants to help him get to Alaska. Alaska, she says, will be the

45

answer to all of their financial woes. Not without guile, Lolita signs her letter "Yours expecting, Lolita." "Expecting" is a pun, for Lolita is both expecting a baby and expecting money from Humbert. Nabokov parodies the classic letter home to the parents in which the writer asks for money, emphasizes poverty and hardship, and, feeling entitled, signs off with expectations.

PART TWO
Chapters 28–36

Humbert now knows Lolita's address because of the postmark on her letter. Determined to murder Dick Schiller, whom he assumes to be the man who stole Lolita from him years earlier, he takes his blue sedan on the road. He pulls over to get target practice. Hanging an old gray sweater on the branch of a tree, he aims and fires, filling the sweater with holes. Then he tosses the sweater in the back of the car, reloads the gun, and goes on his way. In Coalmont, townspeople tell Humbert that Dick Schiller and his wife have moved. One of the women suggests that he try looking in the last house on Hunter Road. The house is a clapboard shack surrounded by weeds.

> "Above all, *Lolita* seems to me an assertion of the power of the comic spirit to wrest delight and truth from the most outlandish materials . . . . [it] brings into grotesque relief the cant, the vulgarity, and the hypocritical conventions that pervade the human comedy."
>
> **CHARLES ROLO**, *ATLANTIC MONTHLY*

Lolita opens the door. She is taller, adorned with pink-rimmed glasses, and enormously pregnant under a brown dress. Humbert loves her still. Lolita cheerfully beckons Humbert in, and Humbert is dazzled by her "Botticelli" beauty. Dick is in the back yard, fixing something. Humbert looks through the kitchen window at Dick and realizes that the young, dark-haired man is not the bald man who stole Lolita from him. He demands that Lolita tell him who she left with. Lolita thought that Humbert knew. She tells him the name, which we do not hear yet, although Humbert says clever readers will know it already.

Lolita says that the man who followed them is the only one she was ever really crazy about. Humbert asks about himself, and she says he was a good father. Lolita had known the man with whom she left before she knew Humbert. He had spoken once to Charlotte's women's club, and kissed her when she was ten. He saw her with Humbert at The Enchanted Hunters inn, where he was writing the play that she would rehearse in Beardsley two years later, and he wrote the play that was performed at the Colorado theater festival she and Humbert attended. "Cue," as she calls man she left with, took her to a dude ranch and expected her to take part in orgies. When she refused, he threw her out. Then she met Dick.

Humbert asks Lolita to come with him. Lolita thinks he means he will only give her the money if she has sex with him. Humbert begs her to spend her life with him, and although she seems moved, she says no. Defeated, Humbert hands her an envelope containing $400 in cash and a check for $3,600. He weeps and again begs her to leave with him, but she refuses, saying she would rather go back to Cue than go back to him.

Driving off in the little blue sedan, Humbert hears Lolita call to Dick. Humbert cries.

Back in Ramsdale, Humbert has little trouble finding the mystery man's address. He goes to talk to Ivor Quilty, who willingly reveals the address of his nephew, Clare Quilty.

Humbert considers telephoning Quilty, but decides to drive up the treacherous Grimm Road and survey Pavor Manor, where Quilty lives.

Humbert goes to Quilty's house during a thunderstorm. No one answers his knock, so Humbert enters and goes upstairs, noting clutter from a recent party, and encounters Quilty, who is wearing a purple silk dressing gown. Apparently, Quilty is alone in the house. Humbert asks Quilty if he recalls a little girl named Dolores Haze. Quilty, who seems to be on drugs, answers illogically and says that Humbert is boring him. He sees Humbert's gun and, unafraid or uncomprehending, continues babbling cheerfully. Humbert tells him to concentrate, to try to focus on Dolly Haze and understand that he is about to die.

Humbert fires toward the floor. Quilty protests that he is almost impotent, and all he did was save Lolita from a "beastly pervert." Humbert asks him if he wants to be executed standing or sitting. Quilty lurches toward Humbert, and the two wrestle. Humbert fires again, eventually hitting Quilty, who complains in a faux British accent that the bullets hurt "atrociously." Humbert reloads, and, as Quilty drags himself from one room to another, shoots Quilty in the head. Quilty, still alive, gets in bed. Humbert shoots him again and then stays with Quilty until he is quiet.

Downstairs, Humbert encounters a number of laughing people who are arriving and helping themselves to Quilty's liquor. "I've just killed Clare Quilty," he

A FRUSTRATING MURDER

The murder of Clare Quilty is one of the most sustained and frustrating murders in literature. Quilty robs Humbert of the dramatic satisfaction he craves, for in his drugged state, he cannot behave seriously or reflect, as Humbert wants him to, on his misdeeds. He is incapable of scripting his exit like a film noir villain, whose last act is to acknowledge his misdeeds. Instead, he dies in an undignified manner—taking several bullets to the head and body while still stumbling around. The murder of Quilty is a grotesque comedy. His friends laugh at him and ignore his bleeding body, and his murderer comes to a stop not in a dramatic squeal of brakes or in a collision, but in a peaceful meadow full of cows.

announces. They jokingly congratulate him, saying someone would have done it eventually. Looking up, Humbert sees Quilty heaving on the landing and finally dying. Quilty's friends, oblivious to the fate of their host, call to him, urging him to hurry.

Humbert leaves. He senses he is being followed, and soon he runs a red light and drives Charlotte's car into a meadow. It comes to a gentle halt amid several "surprised cows." Eventually, police officers take him out of the car.

Humbert writes that he began this story fifty-six days ago in a psychopathic ward and is finishing it in "seclusion." He says, "Had I come before myself, I would have given Humbert at least thirty-five years for rape and dismissed the rest of the charges." He says he wants his memoir published when Lolita is dead. As for his last words to Lolita, he hopes she will be true to her husband, and that she will give birth to a boy. Humbert says that in this memoir, he and Lolita can share immortality.

UNDERSTANDING AND INTERPRETING
Part Two, Chapters 28–36

The Mystery Man Unmasked: Humbert was fairly sure it was Dick Schiller who followed him and Lolita through Colorado and stole Lolita away. However, when Humbert glances out at Lolita's backyard and sees Dick, he realizes he was wrong and must look further for Lolita's abductor. Lolita is coy about revealing the man's name. She gives hints and fills in details, but only when Humbert pretends he is going to leave does she reveal the name. Even if we have realized that Lolita left with Clare Quilty, we do not officially find out until Humbert returns to Ramsdale. Clare Quilty was the man in the Dromes advertisement, the Hollywood writer, the man who wrote a play with the same name as the hotel that Humbert and Lolita stayed in and, we realize, that Quilty himself stayed in, sitting in the shadows and insisting that Lolita was not Humbert's daughter. Clare Quilty is the man who followed Humbert and Lolita, the man who, according to the *Who's Who* article that Humbert reads in the prison library, enjoys traveling and fast cars. Clare Quilty is the co-author of the play that Humbert and Lolita attended at the Colorado theater festival. He was the bald-headed man talking excitedly to Lolita in a furtive moment while Humbert was away from the car, the man whom Humbert spied from a distance. The man on the tennis court who swatted Lolita on the butt with his tennis racket had been sent by Quilty. All the mystery men who plagued Humbert on his journeys were actually one man, Clare Quilty.

Vladimir Nabokov

A Crime of Desperation: Already guilty of child molestation, Humbert now decides to murder Quilty. He wants to serve justice to the man who destroyed his relationship with Lolita. He can never be with Lolita, who now understands that Humbert destroyed her childhood, and the only satisfaction he can attain will come from killing the man who stole Lolita from him. Because Humbert's life is meaningless without Lolita, he reckons, he has nothing to lose by murdering Clare Quilty.

Conclusions

In "On a Book Entitled *Lolita*," which serves as an afterword to the novel, Nabokov writes, "despite John Ray's assertion, *Lolita* has no moral in tow." Nabokov does not ask us to assign guilt or decide which character is good and which bad. He refrains from taking anyone's side, as we can see from the fact that Lolita is not entirely or even mostly a sympathetic character. She toys with Humbert and manipulates him. She fails to demonstrate much intelligence or charm. If Nabokov refuses to glorify the character most authors would naturally portray as a victim, he similarly fails to demonize the character most authors would portray as a villain. Humbert is not repulsive or unreflective. Occasionally, he seems aware of the gravity of his treatment of Lolita. He is lyrical, funny, brilliant, and charming. Humbert and Lolita's relationship is not even definitively that of molester and molested. At moments, they seem like a normal couple, loving and troubled. Nabokov takes our easy assumptions and shakes them, forcing us to see his characters as unique people in a unique, troubling, passionate situation.

> "A fine book, a distinguished book—all right, then—a great book."
>
> **DOROTHY PARKER**, *ESQUIRE*

III

PNIN

Pnin

An Overview

Key Facts

Genre: Comic novel; parody of academia

Date of First Publication: 1953

Setting: 1950s; Waindell College, New England

Narrator: Third person observer; an acquaintance of the characters

Plot Overview: Timofey Pnin, a gentle academic from Russia, teaches literature in a small New England town. Just when he begins to feel settled, academia dismisses him. A new colleague tosses him a tentative offer of employment, but Pnin refuses the offer. He chooses the open road and the company of a small dog whom he recently adopted.

Style, Technique, and Language

Style—Increasing Snobbery: At first, the narrator uses a light, humorous tone to describe Pnin, who seems to be a stock figure often found in movies and fiction: the absent-minded professor. As the novel progresses, however, the narrator's tone becomes increasingly sharp and condescending, and he begins to reveal almost as much about himself as he does about Pnin. The narrator unkindly complains about Pnin, condemning Pnin's socks, his habits, his lectures. The narrator's criticisms mount up, his remarks cut deeper into the frail Pnin, and eventually we find that we are no longer laughing at the little absent-minded professor, who has become a fully fleshed-out man. Instead, we empathize with him and resent the barbed complaints of his snobby judge.

Technique—Mysterious Narrators: The structure of Nabokov's novels is rarely straightforward. He often embeds a mystery in his plots or throws us off balance with an unreliable, difficult narrator. He uses both techniques in *Lolita*, and again in *Pnin*. At first, *Pnin* seems a collection of loose, episodic recollections written by an omniscient (all-knowing) author about an émigré professor of Russian literature at a small Midwestern university. The narrator could even be Nabokov himself. After we read the first two or three chapters, however, it becomes apparent that the narrator is *not* the author. He is a mystery, someone who has played a role in Pnin's life and has strong personal opinions about Pnin. Not until the final chapter does Nabokov reveal the identity of this mystery narrator.

> "There is no question that Nabokov is a terrific stylist. But often I have the feeling that reading him is more a question of witnessing a performance than simply enjoying a book."
>
> **TOM FRENKEL**, *THE COMPULSIVE READER*

Language—Broken English: Pnin's broken English helps make him a sympathetic character, especially when contrasted with the narrator's masterful command of the English language. We cringe at Pnin's bungled attempts to express himself to his students, landlady, or strangers. When we hear Pnin ask, "Where is located the public telephone?" we might think of our own mangled sentence structure in foreign languages.

Characters in *Pnin*

Betty Bliss: A student in Pnin's class. Betty is not a particularly bright student, but she is earnest and affectionate in a quiet, unassuming way. Pnin sees her after she has graduated from college and gotten engaged.

Pnin

Professor Blorenge: The chairman of the French department. Blorenge is stunned when Dr. Hagen, chairman of the German department, suggests that perhaps Pnin might teach a French course. The suggestion is outrageous to Blorenge, because Pnin actually speaks French, which would upset the faculty of the French department. Blorenge himself speaks no French.

The Bolotovs: Liberal Russian intellectuals in their late forties who fled Russia at the time of the Russian Revolution.

Konstantin Chateau: An old friend of Pnin's. In the 1920s, Chateau and Pnin were students together at the University of Prague. Chateau teaches the History of Philosophy at a college in New York. He and Pnin deplore the "typical American college student," who attends college only to receive a degree and then get a job.

Isabel Clements: The daughter of the couple who rent a room to Pnin. After Isabel marries, her parents decide to rent out her bedroom, but when her marriage ends, she comes to reclaim the room.

Joan and Laurence Clements: The married couple who rent a room to Pnin. At first Joan finds Pnin eccentric, but eventually she warms to him, especially after his wife treats him harshly. Laurence distances himself from Pnin until he realizes that Pnin is a goldmine of inspiration for Laurence's Philosophy of Gesture course. He begins filming Pnin's hand movements, shrugs, and other expressions.

Judith Clyde: A member of the Cremona Women's Club. She invites Pnin to speak on a timely topic: "Are the Russian People Communist?" Pince-nez resting on her nose, she instructs the women in the audience on the correct pronunciation of Pnin's name and tells them, inaccurately, that Pnin's father was Dostoevsky's physician.

Gwen Cockerell: The wife of Jack Cockerell, head of the English department. Gwen listens again and again to Jack's impersonations of Pnin and enjoys her husband's mimicry. When she hosts a newly hired Russian instructor, she prepares what she believes the wife of the English department head should serve to a European guest: an English breakfast of fish and kidneys.

Jack Cockerell: The head of the English department. Cockerell is an agitated, nervous, chattering man, dubiously renowned for his lengthy impressions of Pnin.

Vladimir Nabokov

Al Cook: A Russian liberal who fled the Russian Revolution. Al married Susan, whose parents owned The Pines and passed it on to Al and Susan, who host Russian academics at The Pines during the summer. Their guests lounge around, playing croquet and discussing intellectual and literary matters.

Bodo von Falternfels: An Austrian hired while Pnin is away teaching a course in Washington. Because no private office is available, Falternfels moves into Pnin's office, pushing Pnin's desk and books into a dark corner.

> "**P**nin is a comedy of academic manners in a disenchanted world. The central character is our old friend, the absent-minded professor. In Nabokov's hands, however, he becomes a sardonic commentary on the civilization that produced him, a Mr. Chips with the bark on, a Mr. Malaprop cavorting cheerfully among the tragically dispossessed of our time."
>
> **CHARLES POORE**, *THE NEW YORK TIMES*

Dr. Hagen: The dean of the German department. Hagen watches over Pnin, making sure that he is given a sufficient number of classes to justify a full salary. When Hagen is offered a lucrative position at another college, he accepts it and leaves Pnin to fend for himself.

Charles McBeth: A student of Pnin's. Charles has mastered ten languages and is ready to learn ten more. He helps Pnin move his books, typewriter, and sunlamp into Isabel's fluffy pink bedroom.

Dr. Pavin Pnin: Pnin's father. Dr. Pnin, a St. Petersburg ophthalmologist, once treated Leo Tolstoy. He is pleased by his son's successful academic career.

Timofey (Timosha, Tim) Pnin: The hero of the novel. A bundle of eccentricities, Pnin moves to America and learns to speak broken English. America's gadgetry confounds him. Plastic zippers and cars astonish him. Never far from Pnin's mind is his deep love for his former wife, Liza, who has left him and several successive husbands. While many of Pnin's academic colleagues are petty and sinister, Pnin retains his warm innocence and hope.

Praskovia: The "sturdy sixty-year-old woman" who runs The Pines, making sure the guests are fed and provided with clean sheets. She has volcanic energy and dresses in baggy homemade shorts, a matronly blouse, and rhinestones.

Bill Sheppard: One of the brothers who rents an upstairs room to Pnin. Bill is a retired groundskeeper of the college who is totally deaf in one ear. He has never learned to pronounce Pnin's name, which he thinks is "Neen."

Bob Sheppard: One of the brothers who rents an upstairs room to Pnin. When Bob's wife dies, he moves in with his brother, Bill. It is Bob who rushes to Pnin's aid when he falls down the stairs.

Roza Shpolyanski: Another guest at The Pines during Pnin's summer visit. Madame Roza finds Pnin delightful. She is especially pleased by his expert croquet technique, cheering him when he scores a point.

Mrs. Thayer: The librarian of the college. Mrs. Thayer suggests to Pnin that he could find a nice, quiet room of his own at the Clementses' house. She shares a comic moment with Pnin after he receives a notice to return a book to the library because another patron needs it desperately. It turns out that the "other patron" is Pnin himself.

Professor Thomas and Professor Wynn: Pnin cannot tell Professor Thomas and Professor Wynn apart, much to the amusement of his colleagues and the bafflement of the professors.

Eric Wind: The doctor who lures Liza away from Pnin. Although Liza is carrying Eric's child when she returns to Pnin, he gratefully takes her back anyway, and soon they board a ship for America. Eric follows them to America, planning to marry Liza after Pnin has paid for her passage.

Liza Pnin Wind: Pnin's ex-wife. Always unsatisfied with her various husbands, Liza goes through several marriages over the course of the novel. She is brusque with Pnin, who loves her despite her unkindness.

Victor Wind: The son of Liza and Eric Wind, who are both specialists in abnormal psychology. Experts have administered batteries of tests to Victor and found him absolutely normal, which his parents cannot understand. Victor is fond of Pnin, who tries hard to please him despite knowing virtually nothing about children.

Reading *Pnin*

Chapter One

Professor Pnin, a fifty-two-year-old professor of Russian, is on an almost empty railway coach. He has checked his Gladstone traveling bag twice since he boarded the train to make sure that it contains his good black suit, his notes for a lecture on the question "Are the Russian People Communist?", which he will deliver tonight to the Cremona Women's Club, a copy of a talk he will give next Monday ("Don Quixote and Faust"), and an essay written by **Betty Bliss**, a graduate student. The narrator tells us that one of Pnin's students enrolled in Russian because she had heard that simply by learning the Russian alphabet, she could read *Anna Karamazov* in the original Russian.

Pnin wonders about his packing strategy. Should he have put his lecture notes in his suit, which is in the bag, or in the shirt he is currently wearing? His wallet holds two ten-dollar bills, a newspaper clipping, and his certificate of naturalization. The train conductor enters the coach, examines Pnin's ticket, and explains that this train has not stopped at Cremona for two years.

Pnin is incredulous. He says he has an important lecture to deliver and must reach Cremona. The conductor consults a schedule book and suggests that Pnin get off at Whitchurch and catch a bus that departs an hour later for Cremona. Pnin is in utter disbelief, for he meticulously checked the timetable. Often in the past, something beyond Pnin's control shattered his carefully planned life. Now, in this New World, he is still a victim of illogic. Pnin is not aware that the timetable he consulted was published five years ago.

MARY POPPINS'S BAG

If you have seen the 1964 film *Mary Poppins*, you have seen a Gladstone bag such as the one Pnin carries on the train. Mary Poppin's magical Gladstone bag held a limitless supply of unlikely items. Gladstone bags, the story goes, were first carried by the wife of the late-nineteenth-century physician Horace Gladstone. Mrs. Gladstone asked a luggage-maker to fashion her a bag similar to her husband's medical bag, commodious yet light enough for her or her servant girl to carry onboard ships. The bag was an imme-diate hit with other travelers, and by the time the *Titanic* was christened, most of its first-class passengers owned Gladstone bags. The bags have hard bottoms, hinged, metal-frame openings, and double leather handles.

Pnin

Stepping off the train at Whitchurch into an unusually warm October afternoon, Pnin enters the waiting room of a train station, gives his Gladstone bag to a desk clerk, who assures him that he needs no receipt for it, and walks to a nearby coffee shop, where he eats two sandwiches. He has five minutes before the bus to Cremona departs.

When Pnin returns to the station, there is a new desk clerk on duty, and he refuses to give Pnin his Gladstone bag. Pnin sees the bus for Cremona pulling up across the street. He is overcome by anxiety, wondering if he will be able to deliver his speech and receive the $50 compensation. Abandoning his bag, he boards the bus—and realizes that his suit coat pocket holds not his lecture notes, but Betty Bliss's typed essay.

He gets a refund from the driver and walks through a small park, thick with laurels and rhododendrons, and down an alley. He feels nauseous and assaulted by fate. A painful childhood memory begins to engulf him in waves of anxiety. When he was eleven years old, he fell ill with fever, and his mother and a servant wrapped him in medicine-soaked linen, oilskin, cotton, and flannel. Pnin lay in bed staring at a screen decorated with leaves, a squirrel, a hunched old man, and a bridle path. Held tightly in his torturous bindings, Pnin searched unsuccessfully for order in the wallpaper. He could see leaves, rhododendrons, and oak, but could not find the pattern.

Breathing deeply, Pnin rises and walks back to the train station, where the clerk who checked his bag has returned. Smiling, the clerk offers the bag to Pnin and says that two men who are loading a truck nearby are going to Cremona. He suggests that Pnin ask them for a ride.

Later, seated on a dais and dressed in his new black suit, Pnin waits while **Judith Clyde** introduces him to the other ladies. Professor Pnin, she says, hardly needs any introduction. She proceeds to introduce him at length, explaining the pronunciation of his foreign name and assuring the ladies that although they have a long evening before them, it will be a "rewarding" one. She explains that Pnin's father was Dostoevsky's family doctor and that Pnin has traveled on *both* sides of the Iron Curtain.

Pnin's mind drifts. His heart palpitates. He looks into the audience and imagines that he recognizes an aunt, a long-dead sweetheart, and friends—"murdered, forgotten, unrevenged"—all victims of the Russian Revolution. His father and mother smile proudly at him from the audience. The vision disappears, and it is time for Pnin to begin. An old lady begins clapping her hands silently.

Vladimir Nabokov

U N D E R S T A N D I N G   A N D   I N T E R P R E T I N G
Chapter One

Fretful and Nervous: The anxiousness with which Pnin plans his trip and obsesses about the best place to put his notes suggests that he misplaces things and worries excessively about his schedule. Judith Clyde advised Pnin to catch a train that leaves Waindell at 1:52 P.M. and reaches Cremona at 4:17 P.M. To double-check her advice, Pnin obtains an official printed timetable and takes personal responsibility for choosing the correct train to Cremona, unaware that his schedule is five years out of date. Once on the train, he frets about the possibility of losing or forgetting his lecture notes.

Understanding Pnin: For years, we have cheered loveable losers. Charlie Chaplin's Little Tramp, Charles Schultz's Charlie Brown, and Woody Allen's many *nebbish*es are among the humble men we care about, sympathizing with their attempts to suffer life's setbacks with dignity and resolve. Pnin fits into this collection of lovable losers. He is also the prototypical absent-minded professor, another popular figure of literature and film. An intelligent, if bumbling, man, he tries his best to navigate the days smoothly and reacts with anxiousness and astonishment when things go badly.

"Monstrously built farm boys": Nabokov jokes about the ignorance of American college students by mentioning the "languid Eileen Lane," who enrolled in Russian because someone told her that after mastering the Russian alphabet, she could read *Anna Karamazov* in its original language. Whoever Eileen spoke to has confused *Anna Karenina* with *The Brothers Karamazov*, both classics, and made a mishmash of the titles. Eileen also makes the absurd, amusing assumption that simply learning the alphabet of another language results in fluency. While she could read a Russian novel aloud after mastering the Russian alphabet and learning its few phonetic rules, she would not understand a word of what she read. Waindell, a place that encourages students of Eileen's ilk, stands for most American colleges, which are peopled by "monstrously built farm boys and farm girls."

Oblivious Clyde: Nabokov satirizes book club ladies with his character Judith Clyde, a grown woman and a reader who shows herself to be just as ignorant as Eileen Lane. She makes gaffe after gaffe when introducing Pnin to the Cremona Women's Club. She remarks that Pnin's father was Dostoevsky's family doctor, when actually he treated Leo Tolstoy. Judith either does not know the difference between Dostoevsky and Tolstoy, two famous but very different Russian writers, or cannot be bothered to remember the correct information. Judith characterizes Pnin as a man who has "traveled quite a bit on both sides of the Iron Curtain." This is a hilarious, depressing understatement of the facts. Like Nabokov himself, Pnin escaped from the Bolsheviks during the Russian Revolution and later escaped from Hitler's Nazi troops and sailed for America. He has not "traveled" so much as fled death.

Comically Earnest: Pnin has no difficulty laughing at himself, a skill that defuses unhappy or tense situations. Yearly, he tells his students what happened when he first came to America and a U.S. customs official asked if he was or ever had been an anarchist. Ever the philosophical professor, Pnin earnestly asked the man if he was referring to "practical, metaphysical, theoretical, mystical, abstractical, individual, [or] social" anarchism — insulting and confusing the menial clerk, who had no idea what Pnin had asked him. As a result, Pnin was held for two

> "**P**nin is hilariously funny and of a sadness."
>
> **GRAHAM GREENE**, *THE GUARDIAN*

weeks on Ellis Island. Pnin's comical earnestness appears again when he prepares what could have been an explosive speech about Communism. In 1950s America, Communism was an electric topic, and Communists were reviled and feared. So humble and gentle is Pnin, however, that even the title of his speech smoothes out the political tension with humor. The title is "Are the Russian People Communist?", which is a deceptively complicated, funny question. In the popular American imagination, all Russian people, living as they were in a Communist nation, were Communist. From a more objective point of view, however, the actual "people" of Russia, who were suffering Stalin-era oppressions, had had—and had wanted—little to do with the establishment of Communism. Pnin (and Nabokov) had fled the country when the Communists came to power. Pnin himself is one example of a non-Communist Russian.

Panic Attacks: In this novel, Nabokov coins the term "Pninian," which means fussy and fretful. Pnin continually fusses and frets, attempting to make sure his life is always in order. Above all, he wants to protect himself from irrationality and chaos, which constantly threaten to overwhelm him. As a child, Pnin had the sense that if he could see patterns and order, he could gain control of his

Vladimir Nabokov

anxieties. When he had a fever, he searched for order in the decorative panels of wood visible from his bed and in his wallpaper, but could only make out some oak leaves and a tangle of rhododendrons. We know that he now suffers from the same worries that bothered him as a child, for in Whitchurch, he sees a gray squirrel sitting on its haunches, rhododendrons, and an oak-lined alley leading to the station. These repeated images link Pnin's worry-filled past to his present (and thereby make a pattern, although Pnin does not seem to recognize it).

Chapter Two

Winter has set in. **Professor Laurence G. Clements** and his wife, **Joan**, are coping badly with an empty nest. Their only daughter, **Isabel**, has married and moved away. They have decided to rent out their daughter's room, but to their dismay, no one has telephoned to inquire about the room except Professor Pnin, whom Joan calls a "cracked ping-pong ball."

Pnin comes to see the Clementses. He explains in pleading, broken English that the College Home for Single Instructors, where he currently lives, is filled with too many people. Pnin coughs and warns Joan that soon he will have all of his teeth pulled out. Joan leads Pnin upstairs and shows him Isabel's fluffy, pink room and small adjoining bathroom. Pnin agrees to take it, saying he will pay no more than a dollar a day.

That afternoon, **Charles McBeth**, a student of Pnin's, helps move Pnin's belongings, which include an "elaborate sun lamp" (the source of Pnin's perennially tanned bald head), an enormous Russian-alphabet typewriter, and seventy-four library books. Later that evening, Pnin interrupts a small faculty cocktail party downstairs, complaining about the erratic blasts of heat from the floor vents. Joan manages to silence **Jack Cockerell**, the head of the English department, who has been doing an impression of Pnin. The head of the German department, **Dr. Hagen**, offers Pnin a highball.

The next morning, Pnin's dentist extracts his teeth, and ten days later, Pnin radiates an artificial but convincing all-American smile. He is enormously happy. Laurence Clements slowly warms to Pnin and decides to film Pnin's vast array of gestures and shrugs, cataloging them for his popular course on the Philosophy of Gesture. Pnin shows the film to his students of Russian, including dewy-eyed Betty Bliss. Pnin has a soft spot for Betty, but someone else has already claimed his heart—his former wife, **Dr. Liza Wind**, a poet and psychiatrist.

In 1925, when Pnin met Liza in Paris, she was a mermaid-like woman with a snowy complexion, large breasts, and thick ankles. She had just turned twenty and was working in a sanatorium under Dr. Rosetta Stone. Pnin was a sparsely bearded bookstore clerk, and he wrote Liza love letters, which helped her recover from a suicide attempt she had made after a nasty case of unrequited love. Before Pnin married Liza, he told her that he wanted her to have enough time to write poetry and continue her psychiatric research. They married and moved into Pnin's small, shabby apartment, where Liza wrote innumerable forgettable lyrical poems, and finally received praise in a newspaper from a notable literary critic who had been bribed by Liza's lover. Pnin carried the folded newspaper clipping with him for a while.

One day in 1938, Liza telephoned Pnin and said that she was leaving him for a man named **Dr. Eric Wind.** Some time later, an American professor offered Pnin a job in America. Pnin informed Liza about the offer. A few months passed, and Liza, heavily pregnant, returned to Pnin. Pnin was deliriously happy, and planned to adopt the unborn child of Eric Wind. He and Liza boarded a ship for the New World, and Pnin soon discovered that Dr. Wind was also on board. Liza, Wind said, was a "very sick woman," her "pregnancy being the sublimation of a death wish," and yet he planned to marry her. A few days later, the boat docked at Ellis Island. Liza went to live with Dr. Wind, and they eventually married. Recently, the French professor **Konstantin Chateau** sent Pnin an article co-authored by Liza and Eric about group therapy for maladjusted married couples. The article argues that married couples should aspire to be like Siamese twins.

Returning to the present, we learn that Liza has come to visit. She arrives on a Greyhound bus, hugs Pnin's bald head, and exclaims that his new teeth are splendid. En route to Pnin's place, Liza talks about her son with Eric, **Victor,** whom she has just enrolled in a fancy, English-style private school. In Pnin's room, Liza says she has fallen in love with a man named George. Eric knows all about George and has promised to cure her irrational infatuation with him, as long as she continues to sleep with him (Eric). She has agreed to this, but continues to sleep with George, too.

Liza instructs Pnin to call a taxi and asks him to send Victor some pocket money now and then. Pnin is Victor's symbolic "water father," Liza says, just as Eric is Victor's "land father." Eric's cash flow has dried up, and Victor will need money to keep up with the rich boys at his school. Liza's taxi pulls away, and Pnin wanders to a park. A squirrel eyes him and then scampers up a water fountain. Pnin turns the water on, and the squirrel laps at it for several seconds,

Vladimir Nabokov

looking contemptuous, before running away. Pnin wonders if "she"—he could mean Liza or the squirrel—was suffering from a fever. He goes to a bar.

Joan Clements arrives home and is thrilled to find an airmail letter from Isabel. As she reads it, Pnin comes in with tears in his eyes, searching for "viscous" (whiskey) and "sawdust" (soda). Joan distracts him by showing him a magazine ad featuring a sailor and his cat looking at a mermaid. The sailor fantasizes about the mermaid's tail splitting into legs. The cat fantasizes about the mermaid turning into a fish. Pnin lays his head on his arms, sobbing, "I haf nofing left, nofing, nofing!"

UNDERSTANDING AND INTERPRETING
Chapter Two

Reality and Longing: The magazine advertisement that Joan shows Pnin demonstrates how people project their unrealistic desires onto other people, an important theme in the novel. In the ad, sailor and cat are looking at the same mermaid, but the sailor imagines her as a beautiful woman, and the cat imagines her as a tasty fish. In their longings, both sailor and cat take half of the mermaid's real being and combine it with their own fantasies. Liza is initially described as a "limpid mermaid," so we are meant to compare her to the mermaid in the ad and reflect on how Pnin perceives her. During their brief afternoon together, Pnin fantasizes, like the cat or the sailor, that Liza is someone she is not—he imagines that she is a woman worthy of his love.

Differences in Perception: Just as the mermaid is interpreted differently by the cat and the sailor, so Nabokov leaves room for readers to interpret his characters is varying ways. Some of us will think of our own failings when we read about Pnin's bumbling efforts to reconcile with the woman he loves. Others will feel impatient with Pnin's inability to recognize Liza's fraudulence. Some will see Liza as a user and a taker, a woman without talent or feeling who navigates life by manipulating other people. Others will be impressed by Pnin's kindness and inability to think badly of even the most horrible people. Although Pnin recognizes that Liza is cruel and vulgar, he still longs for her. Though he realizes she is using him, he does not feel angry with her. It does not enrage him when she carelessly speaks of her relationships with other men, asks him for money, and then leaves abruptly. He just feels despair.

Our Affection for Pnin: Nabokov makes us sympathize with Pnin and interpret events as he would. Just as Pnin sees Liza as no one else does, we see Pnin as no one else does. Joan Clements calls Pnin a "cracked ping-pong ball," making fun of his bald head and reputation as a slightly dotty eccentric. She also calls him "pathetic." We gather that most of the faculty think Pnin is an odd duck and a suitable butt of jokes. The head of the English department frequently does an imitation of Pnin. We see Pnin differently, admiring his kindness and feeling sympathy for his broken English and earnest attempts to organize his life, and feeling defensive when people make cruel, casual jokes at Pnin's expense.

A Sex-Obsessed Quack: Nabokov believed that Sigmund Freud (1856–1939) was a shallow, sex-obsessed quack. He rejected Freud's sexual explanations for humankind's emotional ills as simplistic. In his 1931 article in the *New Gazette*, a Parisian newspaper, Nabokov hoped to unmask the popular and adored darling of European psychiatric circles. In Chapter Two of *Pnin*, Nabokov has great fun satirizing Liza and Eric Wind, both psychiatrists and disciples of Freud. Their last name, "Wind," is significant, because it suggests the word "windbags," which aptly describes Eric and Linda, who are empty-headed, tiresome talkers. Dr. Wind's interpretation of Liza's pregnancy as "the sublimation of a death wish" is hilariously absurd. So are the Winds' theories, which they propagate in group therapy for maladjusted married couples. Eric and Liza insist that a truly happy married couple should resemble an ideal "group of two"—that is, Siamese twins. Nabokov shoots satiric arrows into the Winds' jumbled hodgepodge of Freudian theories, symbols, and psychology.

Reversing the Rosetta Stone: When Pnin first meets Liza, she is working in a psychiatric sanatorium under the supervision of "Dr. Rosetta Stone, one of the most destructive psychiatrists of the day." The Rosetta Stone, a slab discovered in 1799 and now on display in the British Museum, is the key to our understanding of Egyptian hieroglyphics. It contains identical texts in Greek, Egyptian script, and Egyptian hieroglyphs, and it is a godsend in the quest to understand our past. Nabokov reverses the meaning of this cherished artifact, naming Dr. Rosetta Stone after it but making her a horror of malpractice. Unsurprisingly, Liza flourishes under her.

Chapter Three

Several seasons pass. Pnin has taught Russian at Waindell College for eight years. After packing up and moving almost every semester, searching for the perfect quiet room, Pnin has been settled comfortably with the Clementses for more than a year. Pnin has removed most of the evidence that his room once belonged to Isabel Clements.

For many years, Pnin was nomadic and homeless. After fleeing the Russian Revolution, he settled in Paris, but eventually had to flee when Nazi troops threatened the city. He rented various single rooms, suffering the noise of jack-hammers beyond his windows, banging doors, warbling radiators, nosey neighbors, and drafty windows.

Now that Joan Clements has gone to visit Isabel and Laurence has also been called away, Pnin has the run of the Clementses' house. Walking toward the college, Pnin remembers that he received a notice from the library, urgently asking him to return Volume 18 of the *Sovetskiy Zolotoy Fond Literaturï* because another library patron requests it. Pnin would like to keep the book much longer, but if a true scholar of Russian literature desperately needs it, Pnin will comply. He sighs and goes back for the book.

The narrator says that Pnin, despite his eight years in Waindell, still struggles with the English language. Pnin's Russian is musical, but his English is monstrous. However, he muddles along, coping with his linguistic quirks. Pnin begins his grammar lecture this morning by talking about the famous Pushkin poem whose opening line, "Whether I wander along noisy streets . . ." is used as an example in the grammar book. Pnin keeps reading the poem aloud, translating as he goes: "And where will fate send me . . . death . . . in fight, in travel, or in waves?"

As Pnin waits for his Advanced Class to begin, the narrator tells us about Pnin's office. Three years ago, Pnin was at last given an office of his own. He furnished it with his things, including a faded Turkish rug and a hand-operated pencil sharpener. Pnin left to teach in Washington state for a summer term, and when he returned, he found that an Austrian professor, **Dr. Bodo von Falternfels**, had moved into the office, put all of Pnin's furniture in a dark corner, and installed a stunning stainless-steel desk and swivel chair. Falternfels's fat dog was sleeping on the Turkish rug.

The Austrian still occupies the office today, but the dog is dead. Pnin goes to the library to return the book. As he walks, "a skimpy squirrel" dashes over a piece of sunlit snow and "scrabbles" up a tree, contending with a swarm of pigeons trying to land. In the library, **Mrs. Thayer**, who recommended the

Clementses' available room to Pnin, is sitting at the loan table. Pnin asks her who requested this particular volume. She checks, and discover that Pnin himself requested it. Pnin growls that he meant to ask for Volume 19, not Volume 18. He shuffles off to his private alcove, muttering that he had written down the correct year for Volume 19. Later, writing note cards for his projected short history of Russian culture, Pnin realizes how lucky he is to be at Waindell, among these rows of obscure Russian books and magazines. When he looks up again, it is dinnertime. He leaves the library and walks to a tavern, where he orders ham slices and a bottle of beer. After a second beer, Pnin decides to attend a film on campus. Watching three silent movie shorts and a Soviet documentary film, he weeps, despite the clichéd images. That night, Pnin awakens when he hears car doors slamming and a key in the lock. Isabel Clements has come home to reclaim her room.

UNDERSTANDING AND INTERPRETING
Chapter Three

Searching for a Room: Since Pnin left Russia, he has struggled to secure a satisfactory, steady home for himself. He has conducted a seemingly endless search for a quiet, warm room where he can read and do his research. The room in the Clementses' house is not ideal, but it is good enough. At the least, it means he will not find it necessary to move every semester, as he has done for the eight years he has been in Waindell. All of his security rests in Isabel Clements's pink bedroom. Pnin finds a little literary security in the Clementses' house, too. He is grateful that the Clementses' do not own volumes by Hendrik Willem van Loon and Dr. Cronin, two authors frequently represented on American bookshelves in the 1950s, nor novels translated by the omnipresent Mrs. Garnett. The Clementses' home has become homey to Pnin.

Pnin in Class: When Pnin lectures, he becomes so completely immersed in the joys of the literature that often he does not realize that what he is reading has personal relevance to himself and his melancholy life of wandering and stopping here and there. Pnin's mispronunciations, verbal quirks, and insertions of Russian phrases are delightful. Nabokov's humor often focuses on the fact that the Russian language has no equivalent for English articles (*a, an,* and *the*). Nabokov also plays with the sounds of Pnin's English: Pnin's pronunciation of "hat" sounds like "hot," for example, and his pronunciation of "Joan" like "John." Nabokov, like Pnin, delights in language and constantly uses alliteration, writing of "silvery sun," "primitive perspective," "flabby skin and flapping clothes," and "phony folk songs."

A PASSEL OF BAD WRITERS

Nabokov's introduction to literary America was not a happy one. Having grown up in a country that boasted such masters as Dostoevsky, Tolstoy, Chekhov, and Turgenev, Nabokov was appalled to learn that Americans considered novels second-class literature. According to American conventional wisdom, women read novels and men read pulp westerns. However, Nabokov realized, among the so-called literati of America, certain novels were assigned a measure of recognition—the novels of A.J. Cronin (1896–1981) and Hendrik van Loon (1882–1944), and translations of Russian classics by Constance Garnett (1861–1946). Cronin, people told him, was praiseworthy because he was a doctor and because his main characters struggled with thorny matters of philosophical and cultural significance. Van Loon was supposedly admirable for his two highly praised, everything-you-want-to-know books: *The Story of Mankind* (1921) and *The Story of the Bible* (1923). Judging by Pnin's reaction to Cronin and van Loon, it seems Nabokov was not impressed by either writer. Constance Garnett, the wife of a British librarian, translated many Russian literary masterpieces into English. Nabokov skimmed several of her translations and pronounced them "meretricious"—pretentious, flashy, vulgar, and woefully inaccurate.

Exiled from Everywhere: Pnin seems doomed to be constantly driven out, exiled, expelled. Exiled from Russia, Pnin barely escapes Nazi troops threatening his home in Paris. Now, in America, his exiles are less serious but equally relentless, even if self-imposed. Pnin had hoped to create a small home away from home in his office, but when he returned from a summer teaching in Washington state, he discovered that another professor had taken possession of his office, shoving Pnin's things into a dark corner. Pnin has also felt driven to leave his lodgings time after time. He has moved sixteen times in his eight years in Waindell. After Pnin begins to fit into the routine of the Clementses and they adjust to him, Pnin starts to breathe easy. Just when he feels that he finally has a home, Isabel Clements returns to drive him out and make him homeless once again.

The Symbolism of Squirrels: Squirrels, which have appeared in every chapter to this point, serve various purposes, reminding Pnin of his childhood, showing us Pnin's kindness, and giving us an animal representation of Pnin. In Chapter One, we learned that when Pnin was eleven years old and battling a severe fever, he stared at the panels in his room, one of which depicted a squirrel sitting on its haunches and examining something in its paws. As an adult, similarly dazed, Pnin walked toward a train station and was observed by a squirrel sitting on its haunches and nibbling at a peach pit. In Chapter Two, after Liza leaves Pnin, a squirrel watches Pnin approach a water fountain. The squirrel runs down the tree and leaps onto the basin of the water fountain, waiting. The kindly Pnin pauses and presses the lever, and the squirrel drinks its fill and then skitters away, ungrateful, having taken advantage of Pnin's kindness just as most people do. In this chapter, as Pnin makes his way to the library, "a skimpy squirrel" dashes over the snow, clambers up a tree, and chatters at a swarm of pigeons determined to drive him out. Here, we can identify Pnin with the squirrel, for Pnin is displaced by Isabel just as the squirrel is displaced by the pigeons.

Chapter Four

Victor Wind, fourteen years old and now a student in St. Bartholomew's prep school for boys, has not seen his father, Eric Wind, in two years. Wind is in South America, and Liza, who is about to marry for the third time, lives in Buffalo, New York. When Pnin first started writing to Victor, the second piece of correspondence he sent was a picture postcard featuring a gray squirrel.

Since he was a child, Victor has been a mystery to his parents. He seems to suffer from no neuroses. His parents, experts on neurosis, finally resorted to

JACK LONDON AND COMMUNISM

One of the key reasons for the popularity of Jack London's fiction in Russia was its emphasis on the survival of the fittest, an emphasis at odds with the Communist ethos. Russian political propagandists could point to London's doctrine of survival of the fittest as an apt metaphor for the fate of the average individual living in the United States. It served the purposes of Russian propagandists to portray the United States as a harsh, cruel place where only the strong survive. Under Russian Communism, in theory, everyone worked for the good of all, and the government made sure that everyone was taken care of. In contrast, in the U.S., according to Communist propagandists, everyone was out for himself, ready to do in anyone who competed for a job or a crust of bread, and fat-cat capitalists thrived on profits from underpaid workers laboring in assembly lines. Although the main characters in London's popular novels were often dogs or wolves, the symbolism was clear to the Russian propagandists: in order to survive in Jack London's America, one had to live by the law of the club or the fang.

Freudian role-playing. They hoped to ease Victor into the painful but inevitable Oedipus phase, wherein he would long to "re-enter" his mother and castrate his father. Victor was not interested in doing either.

Fixated on heredity, Liza and Eric searched their family trees to explain the genesis of Victor's artistic talents. As a small child, Victor did not scribble but drew perfect circles and rectangles. Eric and Liza subjected Victor to the Godunov Drawing-of-an-Animal Test, the Fairview Adult Test, the Kent-Rosanoff Absolutely Free Association Test, the Bièvere Interest-Attitude Game, and the Augusta Angst Abstract Test, among others. Each proved that Victor could not be crammed into a psychological pigeonhole. In prep school, Victor enjoyed painting the reflections he saw in the panels of an automobile—gray clouds or a house, for example. He was particularly fond of drawing objects as he observed them through a glass of water: a red apple became a "red band," a black comb turned the water to a "zebra cocktail." Unbeknownst to the Winds, only one thing besides art interests Victor: his correspondence with Pnin. Now, at last, Victor is going to take a bus to meet the great scholar Professor Timofey Pnin, who teaches at Waindell College, some 300 miles northwest of St. Bart's.

On the day before Victor's arrival, Pnin goes shopping, planning to buy Victor a soccer ball, as Americans call it. Pnin uses the European term for soccer ball, *football*, which confuses the clerk helping him. Only after Pnin mimes the shape of the thing he wants does the clerk understand. Pnin also wants to buy Victor a book called *Martin Eden*. The bookstore clerk is puzzled by this title. She wonders if Pnin is referring to a biography of the British statesman Anthony Eden. Pnin tells her that the novel was written by Jack London. The clerk's husband, Mr. Tweed, helps. The bookstore has only a rather dog-eared copy of London's *The Son of the Wolf*. Pnin is utterly puzzled. In Russia, everyone knows and reads Jack London, including little children.

Disappointed, Pnin decides to buy *The Son of the Wolf*. Back at home, Pnin notices a telegram that says Victor will be twenty-four hours late. Victor, along with a few other boys, was caught smoking. Victor eventually arrives. Over a late dinner, Pnin says that Victor should probably call Pnin Tim. He expresses amazement that all Americans are on a first-name basis almost immediately. Pnin is disappointed to see that Victor has not finished his veal cutlet, and he is further disappointed when he finds that Victor hates football and is not particularly skillful at any sport. At home, Pnin introduces Victor to his deaf landlord, old **Bill Sheppard**, and Bill's brother, **Bob Sheppard**. Pnin goes upstairs to get rid of the soccer ball, which Victor does not know he purchased. Bill Sheppard is talking when Victor and Bob hear a crash on the stairway. They find Pnin lying on his back. He smiles and tells Victor about a similar incident in a story of Tolstoy's.

Upstairs, Victor discovers a wrapped book and a $10 bill. (Pnin tossed the soccer ball out the window.) Victor opens *The Son of the Wolf* and says he thinks he will like it. He yawns, which reminds Pnin of Liza. Pnin remembers happy times attending parties with Liza. That night, rain pours down. Despite the pain in his back, Pnin falls asleep, dreaming of fleeing from rabid Bolsheviks. The Sheppard brothers cannot sleep. Victor falls asleep almost immediately, his head under his pillow.

UNDERSTANDING AND INTERPRETING
Chapter Four

Satirizing the Freudians: In this chapter, Nabokov again satirizes Freud and his theories, which hold that sexuality is the genesis for all personality and behavior. In this chapter, Nabokov mocks Freud's idea that all humans, while growing up, pass through an Oedipal stage. In the ancient Greek play *Oedipus Rex* by Sophocles, an oracle prophesies that Oedipus will kill his father and marry his mother. Oedipus is abandoned, found by two shepherds, brought to Corinth, and raised as a prince. He is never told of the prophecy, but when he is an adult, he ventures off on his own. He slays King Laius, not knowing that the king is his father. Later, he marries Laius's widow, Jocasta, who bears him four children, unaware of their blood relationship. When Jocasta and Oedipus learn the truth, Jocasta hangs herself, and Oedipus blinds himself. Freud believed that to reach healthy sexual maturity, all boys must go through the Oedipal stage, in which they symbolically kill their fathers and marry their mothers. Nabokov believed the theory to be rubbish. He was also disgusted by Freudians who insist that the theory applies to every single child, even when the child in front of them obviously defies the theory's predictions. Nabokov makes a wry literary joke by having Pnin, as homeless as the poor infant Oedipus, given shelter by two "shepherds"—Bill and Bob Sheppard.

Inkblots and Inventories: Nabokov's distaste for psychology surpassed what he interpreted as Freud's perversion of classic Greek literature. He scoffed at the multitude of popular psychological tests that parents and teachers administered to children in order to ferret out personality disorders and assess coping abilities and behavior. Nabokov invents humorous names for these tests, like the Augusta Angst Abstract Test. The names of the actual tests almost parody themselves—for example, the Incomplete Sentence Blank, the Thematic Apperception Test, the Bricklin Perceptual Scales, the Perception of Relationship Test, the Millon Clinical Multiaxial Inventory, the Derogatis Psychiatric Rating Test, the Keirsey Temperament Sorter, and the ubiquitous Minnesota Multiphasic Personality Inventory Test. Nabokov portrays Liza and Eric as idiots brainwashed by their own psychiatric training. They are experts in abnormal behavior so swept up in theory that their normal child seems abnormal to them. The idea that Victor has no neuroses makes them panic.

Good with Kids: Pnin has almost no experience with children, but he treats Victor with respect, and eagerly tries to please him with thoughtful gifts. While Pnin and Victor eat a late supper, Pnin talks to Victor exactly as he would to a classroom of students. He affectionately confesses that he does not understand the American habit of immediately calling slight acquaintances by first names. Pnin says America amazes him, and that while he adores its gimmicks—especially zippers and plastic gadgets—he probably will never master its language. When Victor mentions hating soccer, he does not mean to hurt Pnin's feelings. Victor has no idea that Pnin bought him a soccer ball as a present. Although the misstep pains Pnin, he realizes that he does not want to give Victor a present he will dislike. His willingness to discard the present to avoid embarrassing Victor shows generosity and selflessness, key qualities in dealings with children.

Shadow-tail: Squirrels figure again in this chapter, this time to show the natural affinity of Victor and Pnin. When Pnin first started writing to Victor, the second item he sent was a picture postcard of a gray squirrel. The postcard pleased Victor, and he was happy to learn that the word "squirrel" comes from a Greek word meaning "shadow-tail." This is exactly the kind of information that also pleases Pnin.

Chapter Five

Pnin has received and accepted an invitation to spend the summer of 1954 at The Pines, the rambling country home of a fellow Russian émigré. Pnin points his "pale blue, egg-shaped" sedan northeast. Despite taking lessons at the Waindell Driving School and studying the driver's manual while lying in bed nursing his sore back, Pnin's driving skills are even worse than his sense of direction. He does not understand why he should stop for a red light, for example, when neither car nor people are in sight.

Pnin has a treacherous drive, but at last arrives at The Pines. Pnin's host, **Al Cook,** has been in America for twenty years. He is "kindly" and guileless, dressing exactly like what he is: an American business executive, a Mason, and a golfer. When Al and his wife Susan discovered they would never have children, they decided to invite several elderly Russians for even-numbered summers, and elderly Americans for odd-numbered summers. Most of the guests this year are educated liberals who left Russia soon after the Revolution. They spend the summer sitting in the shade of trees, talking about literature, lying in hammocks reading Russian-language newspapers, and sipping tea. Occasionally, parents bring bored college-age children with them. Members of the younger generation know no Russian and have no interest in their parents' backgrounds.

> "Twentieth-century Russian literature has produced nothing special except perhaps one novel and two stories by Andrei Platonov, who ended his days sweeping streets."
>
> **JOSEPH BRODSKY**

Al and Susan Cook attend mostly to host-and-hostess duties. The task of feeding and bedding the summer assortment of guests falls to **Praskovia**, a stocky, sixty-year-old "woman of the people," who usually dresses in shorts, a "matronly blouse," and rhinestones. Occasionally, she is helped by her husband, an amateur bookbinder addicted to his hobby.

The **Bolotovs** and **Roza Shpolyanski** watch Pnin's arrival. Pnin, moving at only ten miles an hour, clutches the steering wheel. Varvara Bolotov claps her hands as Pnin steps out of the car wearing a bright green sport shirt. Bolotov lumbers forward to shake Pnin's hand, exclaiming that he is reading *Anna Karenina* for the seventh time and has discovered that Tolstoy did not know on which day the novel begins. Pnin announces that the day was Friday, February 23, 1872, by the New Style calendar.

Pnin greets his friend **Konstantin Chateau**, who teaches at a large New York university. Chateau and Pnin walk and talk about Russian history, the fate of European teachers abroad, and their dismay at the lack of academic curiosity among "typical American college student[s]." Chateau confesses that he is likely to have an "exploratory" operation on his stomach. Pnin jokes that doctors are often confused when they X-ray him and discover a "shadow behind his heart." "Good title for a bad novel," jokes Chateau. Upon meeting Gramineev, a bald guest who needs a hat so that he can paint atop a knoll without burning his head, Pnin expertly twist the corners of his handkerchief into a knot and fashions a cap to shield Gramineev's head. Pnin tells Chateau that he wanted Victor to come to The Pines, but Liza insisted that her son travel to California.

When they reach the stream, Pnin throws off his bathrobe, revealing the tan he has from sitting in front of his suntanning contraption. He removes a Greek cross on a chain from around his neck and hangs it on a nearby twig, confessing that he wears it only for sentimental reasons. After dinner, the guests play croquet, one of Pnin's favorite childhood sports. He wins, cheered on by **Madam Shpolyanski**, who is thrilled to see Pnin make the shot known as a Hong Kong.

That evening, Pnin hears the sound of jazz from a radio and remembers Mira, a girl from his youth whom he seldom allows himself to think about. Mira married a fur dealer and died in a concentration camp during World War II. Pnin rises and goes outside to walk beneath the pines.

UNDERSTANDING AND INTERPRETING
Chapter Five

A Difficult Journey: The paragraphs dealing with Pnin's attempt to drive a car are a comic *tour de force*. Pnin is thoroughly lost, struggling somewhere in limbo between Waindell and The Pines, dust rising around his little sedan, totally baffled by the directions he got from a filling station clerk.

Intellectuals in Exile: In part, Nabokov creates the scenes of Russian-American professors, relaxed and enjoying the leisure to talk about politics or literature, as an elegant counterpart to Pnin's anemic, whining, sarcastic colleagues at Waindell. The Russians at The Pines are also meant to demonstrate the sadness of people in exile. Their children do not want to be with them or hear their stories; some of their colleagues are unaccounted for; their adopted home sometimes seems strange to them. These émigrés are liberal intellectuals, their precious educations so threatening that they angered the revolutionaries. Now, in America, they teach students who have no understanding of the value of education. The new world could not be more different from the old.

A Good Heart: Pnin is a generous, good-hearted soul. In this chapter, when he sees Gramineev dangerously exposed to the sun, he immediately offers up a large red handkerchief for Gramineev's protection. Pnin is keenly interested in sharing his enthusiasm for whatever bits of literature he can introduce to his beginner Russian classes, even though his degree was not in literature but in sociology and political economy. He is generosity incarnate when dealing with Liza. Before he married her, for example, he assured her that he supported her poetic and psychiatric endeavors. After Liza had left him for Eric Wind and then returned, very pregnant, he welcomed her back with open arms, just as she assumed he would. Pnin even plays host to Liza's son, Victor, and does his best to please the adolescent boy, buying him thoughtful presents and writing to him. In the depths of sorrow, Pnin still thinks of others—even when those others are squirrels. Pnin has none of the pettiness or unkindness that taints almost everyone else in Waindell.

Chapter Six

The fall semester begins. Professors lecture from yellowed notes, graduate students bend over dissertations that no one will read, the English department continues to assume that Galsworthy and Dreiser are great writers, and unpublished faculty members review colleagues' books.

Although Pnin does not know this, next year Professor Hagen, head of the German department, will leave to accept a lucrative professorship at Seaboard University. Hagen is concerned about Pnin, who, as the only Russian professor, has been attached to the German Department. Hagen feels certain that when Falternfels (Pnin's office mate) becomes head of the German department, he will fire Pnin. **Professor Blorenge**, chairman of the French department, who flaunts his inability to speak French, is a professed anti-Pninist and refuses to let Pnin be affiliated with the French department.

Meantime, Pnin is happy. He has rented a small, "cherry-red" brick house, his first real home in thirty-five years. The little brick house is quiet. It has lilacs, an open porch, and occasional pheasants in the yard. The university has raised Pnin's salary. Pnin has invited Professor Hagen, the Clementses, the Thayers, **Professor Wynn**, and Betty Bliss to a housewarming party.

On the night of the party, Pnin wears a luxurious blue silk smoking jacket that he bought at a charity bazaar twenty years ago. Betty Bliss graduated a few years ago. Nnevertheless, she arrives an hour early to help Pnin prepare. Betty shyly displays an engagement ring with a miniscule diamond. She still wears her hair coiled around her head, as she did during her undergraduate days. Betty and Pnin set out French bread, caviar, shrimp, and savory tarts. Along with other drinks is Pnin Punch, a mixture of wine, grapefruit juice, and maraschino cherries served in a large glass bowl that was a surprise present from Victor.

Pnin

Guests begin arriving. Pnin welcomes the ladies gallantly. Joan Clements mentions that **Professor Thomas**, whom Pnin has confused with a Professor Wynn, recently received a grant. Thomas wonders if he will be able to travel abroad now that Senator McCarthy is investigating the political backgrounds of college professors. Dr. Hagen arrives and holds aloft a bottle of vodka. He is cautioned to hide it, lest word reach Senator McCarthy that Hagan possesses a potable from behind the Iron Curtain.

Pnin and his guests discuss the beauty of the large glass bowl and then talk about Cinderella's glass slipper. Pnin tells them that in the original French fairy tale, the slipper was made of squirrel fur.

Alcohol loosens tongues. Even Mrs. Thayer begins mimicking two of her colleagues. Hagen warns Pnin to keep his distance from a particularly scandalous morsel of gossip that is being discussed. Professor Hagen pronounces that phonograph records on every subject should be available to students. He says that students do not even want to listen to Pnin's wonderful personality. Margaret Thayer protests that the personality of a lecturer is important, but Hagen says the world wants machines, not Pnins.

Walking back across campus after the party, the couples discuss Pnin and his verbal oddities. Once alone with Hagen and her husband, Joan says she has never seen Pnin so happy. In fact, she says, he is thinking of buying the house. Hagen returns to Pnin's and asks if he might have a last cup of wine. He then tells Pnin that he is leaving, and consequently Pnin will not be rehired next year. Waindell has no Russian department, and neither the French nor the German department plans to hire Pnin. Hagen says that an old friend of Pnin's has been hired by the English department, and he might assign Pnin a few classes.

Pnin says that although he has been friends with this man for over thirty years, he could never work under him. Hagen finishes his drink and advises Pnin to go to bed with a good mystery novel. Things will seem better tomorrow. Alone, Pnin scrapes scraps from the plates into a brown paper bag, a treat for the little white stray dog that seems to have adopted him. He carefully lowers silverware, glasses, and the big punch bowl into a deep sink of soapsuds. While washing up, Pnin accidentally lets a nutcracker slip from his hands. He hears an excruciating crack of broken glass. Tears filling his eyes, Pnin reaches down, hoping desperately that Victor's bowl has not been broken. The bowl is intact. The nutcracker broke a goblet. Pnin dries everything, then sits down at the kitchen table and begins writing a letter to Hagen.

MAD JOE McCARTHY

On February 9, 1950, Wisconsin's Senator Joseph McCarthy (1908–1957) made an electrifying speech in Wheeling, West Virginia, stating that he had a list of Communists in the State Department. By July, McCarthy was a major political force. In the summer of 1951, he gave a speech attacking the career of the distinguished World War II hero General George Marshall. In 1953, he became Chairman of the Committee on Government Operations, and the following year, he began holding televised "trials," attempting to ferret out people whom he considered "card-carrying" Communists, including government workers, senators, university professors, writers, actors, and playwrights. He was responsible for destroying hundreds of careers and blacklisting hundreds of people. No one—not even the U.S. president or the press—was willing to stand up to McCarthy or criticize his yearlong witch hunt. Only when a television journalist named Edward Murrow accused McCarthy of fraudulent activities and lack of humanity did national sentiment began to turn against McCarthy. McCarthy's hearings, although brief, remain one of the most shameful episodes in modern U.S. history.

UNDERSTANDING AND INTERPRETING

Chapter Six

Yet Another Loss: Throughout the novel, the narrator has chronicled all the losses in Pnin's life. Pnin lost his homeland, Russia, his secure home in France, and his many apartments. All he wants is a quiet refuge from the world where he can do his research. He lost his private office, he lost his comfortable bedroom in the Clementses' house. He lost Liza, his wife. He lost the hope of raising a baby as his son. Now, when he believes that he has finally found a home for himself where he can continue his research and have some peace and quiet, he loses that. His cold, treacherous colleagues turn their backs on him, robbing him of professional stability.

Scorn for Academics: Nabokov has little sympathy for passive, uncurious Waindell students, but he has even less regard for Waindell's professors. Professor Thomas, at least, champions the right of students to argue with each other in class. And Hagen, the head of the German department, deplores the tragedy that students prefer records to instructors with quirky and wonderful personalities. But Clements is horrified that professors would allow students to fill a class period with talking. Blorenge, head of the French department, cannot even speak French and proudly flaunts his ineptitude. We hear that the English department is essentially a sick ward filled with whining hypochondriacs. One of the most hilarious examples of Nabokov's satire focuses on the enormous college mural with badly rendered likenesses of various Waindell professors receiving torches of knowledge from such intellectual giants as Aristotle, Shakespeare, and Pasteur and passing on the torches to representative Waindell students.

> "*Pnin* is the only novel that Nabokov ever published with the traditional disclaimer that any resemblance to living persons was purely coincidental. The book is teeming with people from Cornell, and some of the cutting stories and portrayals are close enough to reality."
>
> **ANDREW FIELD**, *THE LIFE AND ART OF VLADIMIR NABOKOV*

Vladimir Nabokov

Lucky Squirrel Slipper: In *Pnin*, squirrels sometimes function as harbingers, although it is debatable whether they are harbingers of good or evil. When Pnin and the ladies discuss the beauty and great worth of the large glass bowl Victor sent Pnin, the subject of Cinderella's glass slipper comes up. Pnin explains that in the original French fairy tale, the slipper was not glass at all, but squirrel fur. One could argue that the appearance of squirrels means bad luck, for in this chapter, after the mention of squirrels, Pnin learns that he is to lose his job and therefore his house. However, the same incident could also lead one to argue that the appearance of squirrels means good luck. Because everything always goes wrong for Pnin, we assume that the loud crack of glass means that he has accidentally broken the beautiful glass bowl from Victor. In a stroke of good fortune, the breaking glass was just a goblet.

Chapter Seven

Until the final chapter of the novel, the narrator has remained unidentified. Now, however, he tells the story of himself and Pnin. The narrator was once a schoolboy living in St. Petersburg. While riding a beautiful new bicycle one day, something painful got stuck in his eye. The narrator and his tutor sought out the leading ophthalmologist in the city, **Dr. Pavel Pnin**. After the black speck was removed from the narrator's eye, Dr. Pnin's thirteen-year-old son arrived. The narrator remembers Timofey Pnin's crew cut hair, "puffy pale face," and "red ears." He also remembers hearing the doctor praising Timofey's A-plus on an algebra examination. He remembers a map of Russia on the wall, books on a shelf, and a stuffed squirrel.

Five years later, Timofey Pnin happened to stage a play on the property of the narrator's old aunt. The narrator was compelled for some reason to attend the play, along with vacationers and disabled soldiers from a nearby hospital. Pnin played the role of a betrayed husband, flinging a stack of love letters in the face of his wife's lover. In the early 1920s, at a cafe in Paris, the narrator found himself shaking the hand of Timofey Pnin, who was by then the author of several published works on Russian culture. He reminded Pnin of their encounters, but Pnin denied everything, emphasizing that his marks in algebra were always low and insisting that he played the part of a father in the play, not the wronged husband.

On that same day in Paris, the narrator was drawn to a strikingly good-looking young woman who turned out to be Liza Bogolepov. Liza was flirting with a hairy composer, and her lover seemed miserable. Liza asked the narrator if she could send him some of her poems. When they arrived, the narrator found them utterly trite, lacking both talent and originality. He immediately wrote to Liza that her poems were bad and she should stop writing. Later, he ran into her and again she asked him to read her poems. He found them even worse than he remembered. They engaged in a messy affair. Eventually the narrator heard that Liza, distressed over their relationship, had tried to kill herself by taking sleeping pills. Two weeks later, he saw her in a little garden, and she showed him a hand-written proposal of marriage that she had received. Liza asked the narrator to read it over. She would wait until midnight, she said, and if she had not heard from him by then, she would accept the proposal.

The author of the proposal vowed everlasting love to Liza. He said he wanted only to give her a life that would enable her to write her poems. He also wanted her to continue her studies in psychiatry, although he himself did not understand the field of study. He said he was sending her a pamphlet, written by his friend Professor Chateau, which brilliantly refuted a theory proposed by one of Liza's colleagues. This theory claimed that childbirth was tantamount to suicide on the part of a newborn. The letter's author called Liza's attention to an "obvious misprint" in the article, which he had taken the liberty of correcting.

Six years later, the narrator went back to Paris and learned that Pnin had married Liza. Later, at a party the narrator attended, Pnin engaged in a political discussion, and the narrator talked with Liza, who confessed that she had told Pnin "everything" and that Pnin forgave the narrator. One night when Pnin and the narrator were at a gathering, Pnin erupted, insisting to their host that the narrator was a liar who made up stories that they were schoolmates and that Pnin cheated on examinations. Pnin characterized the narrator as "a dreadful inventor."

The narrator recalls being on a New York City bus with Pnin after a social and academic function. Pnin looked healthy and fairly prosperous. He was more assertive than he used to be, regaling the narrator with a long list of instances in which Homer and Gogol use the so-called Rambling Comparison structural narrative.

When the narrator decided to accept a position at Waindell, he wrote to Pnin and asked if he would like to assist him in the special Russian division that he hoped to create. Pnin answered that he was through with teaching and was not even waiting until the end of the spring term to resign. He mentioned that Victor was living in Rome with Liza, who was now married to an Italian art dealer. Pnin closed his note by expressing regret that he would be leaving Waindell a few days before February 15, when the narrator was scheduled to deliver a lecture.

The narrator arrives in Waindell on February 14. Jack and Gwen Cockerell meet him and give him a late supper at their home. Jack impersonates Pnin, a performance that lasts over two hours. He parodies Pnin eating, teaching, eyeballing a comely "coed," confusing the names of colleagues, talking about learning to drive, and being "shot" (fired) by academia. Despite the fact that Gwen has probably sat through the performance numerous times, she brays so loudly with laughter that their brown cocker spaniel begins to sniff the narrator. On a whim, Jack Cockerell decides to call Pnin, just to see if he has left town. There is no answer. Curious, the narrator also decides to call. This time Pnin answers, trying to disguise his voice, and says Pnin has left.

The next day, the narrator sees a small, pale-blue sedan coming up the street, piled high with bundles and luggage. A small white dog is looking out one of the windows. The narrator waves, then trots up the hill to try to hail Pnin at a red light. The driver, wearing a cap with ear flaps and a storm coat, looks straight ahead. The dog yaps, and the little blue car surges forward, passing a beer truck and launching itself upward onto a shining road leading away from Waindell. The narrator trudges home and sits down to a British breakfast of kidneys and fish that Gwen Cockerell has prepared. Jack is anxious to launch into another round of his Pnin impersonations, this time re-creating the night that Pnin addressed the Cremona Women's Club and discovered that he had brought the wrong lecture.

UNDERSTANDING AND INTERPRETING
Chapter Seven

The Narrator Unveiled: For someone who probably grew up on a wealthy estate outside of St. Petersburg, before the Russian Revolution, the narrator has an astonishing command of English. His command of the language contrasts startlingly with Pnin's. It is the arch tone of the narrator's finely honed English that reveals the most about the narrator's character. The narrator is almost too clever. His wordplay is ingenuous—often at the expense of the natural flow of a sentence. During the course of the novel, we may often wish that he would halt his editorializing and let us enjoy the story. Our longing is futile. As the narrator describes how Pnin is dressed, for example, he cannot help harping on Pnin's sloppy, garish socks, his flamboyant tie, and his not wholly successful attempts to Americanize himself. As Nabokov intends, we begin to discount the censorious tone of the narrator and focus more carefully on the person of Pnin himself, perhaps even ignoring the narrator's intrusive "O, careless reader!" gasps.

Sympathizing with the Underdog: The narrator's attitude of superiority toward Pnin causes us to sympathize even more with Pnin. When the narrator points out that the textbook Pnin uses was authored by a fraud, we do not scoff at Pnin, we realize that he offers his students something more valuable than a textbook— he offers them an instructor with a genuine love of literature. Pnin's degrees are in political science and sociology, but like many Europeans of his generation, Pnin has a fierce love of literature, and he shares this excitement for literature with his students, along with unpretentious digressions about his life in Russia and his life since the Revolution. Almost all the other faculty we meet take pains to distance themselves from students and even from their subject matter, disdainful of their students' ignorance. Not Pnin. He fills their minds with his zest for living and for learning. The other professors and even the narrator may feel superior to Pnin, but we come to love him, and we love him all the more *because* of his colleagues' superior airs.

An Unreliable Narrator: In Chapter Seven, we discover that the narrator of this novel is possibly untrustworthy. Despite the fact that Pnin agrees that the narrator is his friend, he insists that he would never work under him. The narrator admits that Pnin called him a "terrible inventor." We learn that the narrator comes to Waindell just as Pnin leaves. The two men never talk to each other in Waindell, which means that the narrator could not have heard a first-hand account of Pnin's doings. Can we trust anything the narrator says, including his portrait of Pnin? He might have reason to feel resentful toward Pnin. After all, the novel implies that Liza and the narrator were having an affair. When Liza asked the narrator to read the letter and respond to her by midnight, the implication was that she wanted the narrator to state his intentions. If he didn't, she would marry Pnin. So the narrator likely has a personal tie to Pnin that makes him somewhat less than objective.

A Lovable Pnin: Whatever the narrator's tie to Pnin, and however he wanted us to perceive the bumbling professor, in the end he represents Pnin as a most lovable, wonderful man. The narrator probably fashions his portrait of Pnin from his own memories and recollections and from the memories and recollections of people who knew Pnin. The result is curiously similar to the portrait of an automobile that Victor Wind saw. Victor imagined the body of the car as separate curves and panels, and then saw what was reflected in those panels and sections. Nabokov, through the narrator, has employed a similar technique, taking the general outlines of Pnin's personality, its curves and panels, and filling them with the reflections and recollections of Pnin's colleagues, former students, and old friends. This portrait does not make us guffaw at Pnin as his colleagues do. Instead, we feel affectionate and protective, smiling at his struggles with his car, his lodgings, and his language.

A Moment of Triumph: The narrator has made Pnin so sympathetic that when Pnin refuses to wait until the end of the term to be officially dismissed, when he packs up his car with his boxes and bundles and the dog that loves him and heads away, we cheer for him. Pnin is departing on his own timetable, leaving the sinister world of Waindell academia behind. He has mastered the car, at least for the moment, making it swish past a truck. He has found a companion. He seems to have a plan. His departure is a moment of triumph. Pnin casts off the confines of Waindell and is reborn, determined to begin again. Pnin's oblivious immunity to the jibes of others, his ability to live in bad conditions, and his proven record as a survivor bode well for his success.

A Sudden End: The novel ends abruptly. Pnin ignores the narrator and escapes in his little blue sedan from the stagnant lives of Waindell academics. Jack Cockerell has slept well and is now ready to launch into yet another impersonation extravaganza, this one about Pnin bringing the wrong lecture notes to a women's club that he was hired to address. Pnin has escaped, but with the mention of these lecture notes, the people of Waindell have come full circle, returning to the beginning of the story. Meanwhile, Gwen Cockerell is busy with an impersonation of her own, preparing a pseudo-British breakfast of "depressing kidney and fish." The Cockerells are a stale, sad couple, but oddly, it is Jack Cockerell who will probably give Pnin a measure of immortality. Pnin is gone, but Jack will continue impersonating him, to the applause and laughter of his colleagues. Pnin's firing seemed like a defeat at first, but in the last chapter we see that the good humor, grit, and freedom belong to Pnin and have fled town with him. He has lost nothing by leaving Waindell. The academics have lost him, and are left with mean-spiritedness and boredom. Hope rides with Pnin and his little white stray dog as they charge forward to tackle a new life.

Conclusions

Pnin confirms the wisdom of standing back from first-person narrators and regarding their reliability with suspicion. Our narrator does not admire Pnin, who strikes him as a harmless figure of fun. The narrator admires himself, a suave Russian with a formidable mastery of the English language. The narrator disdains Pnin's flashy American clothes, his obsession with the year-round suntan, and his dazzling, all-American smile. But just as Nabokov intends, the narrator's elitist sarcasm highlights Pnin's sensitivity. We admire Pnin's virtues: he is devoted to his horrible former wife, he is tender and sensitive and childlike, he is charmingly hopeless with gadgets and cars, he has dearly-held scholarly ambitions, he respects his students, and he loves literature. Poverty and bad luck do not best him. He is superior to his academic colleagues who dislike him or mock him. He does not have their ability to sneer. He has something much better: a good heart and a zest for life.

IV

PALE FIRE

Pale Fire

An Overview

Key Facts

Genre: Fictional scholarship; post-modern novel

Date of First Publication: 1962

Setting: The 1950s in a college town in Appalachia; the 1930s and 1940s in Zembla, a northern country near Russia

Plot Overview: Charles Kinbote, a professor at Wordsmith College, tells us that he has edited the last poem of John Shade, his colleague and friend.

Shade's poem is written in four cantos. After the text of the poem, Kinbote has furnished lengthy notes that purport to analyze the poem, but actually tell a story about Kinbote and Charles the Beloved, deposed King of Zembla. They also explain that an assassin was hired to kill Kinbote, but instead killed Shade.

Style, Technique, and Language

Nabokov's novel has a unique structure. It features a 999-line poem by John Shade and copious commentary on that poem by Shade's neighbor, Charles Kinbote. Shade's poem seems to be about his life, but according to Charles Kinbote, it references—or at least should reference—King Charles the Beloved's escape from Zembla. In *Pale Fire*, Nabokov satirizes flamboyant homosexuals, academic poets who do bland work, and their critic-peers who write annotated volumes on their friends' creative productions. Nabokov also writes of explosive Eastern European politics, Freudianism, self-absorption, middle-class America in a small-college-town setting, the search for meaning by misguided intellectuals, and the role of chance.

Characters in *Pale Fire*

Disa: The Duchess of Payn in Kinbote's story. Making a bad mistake, Disa marries Charles the Beloved, King of Zembla. Charles is a homosexual who has a voracious sexual appetite for page-boys, footmen, gardeners, palace guards—anyone but Disa. Disa eventually exiles herself to a villa in Nice.

> "*Pale Fire* is not only a whodunit but a who-wrote-it. There isn't, of course, a single solution, but the novel is a masterpiece that imprisons us inside its maze-like, multiple plot lines."
>
> **JANET PARKER**, *BOOK BEAT*

The Gardener: Kinbote's gardener. He heroically saves Kinbote from Gradus, a hired assassin from Zembla. Kinbote promises to fund the young black gardener's education. The gardener is impotent, but Kinbote is grateful merely to watch him work shirtless with shovel and hoe.

Gradus (Jack Grey): The man hired to kill Charles the Beloved. A bungler from birth, Gradus first fails to shoot a Charles look-alike in a hospital and then fails to shoot Charles Kinbote, killing Shade instead.

Charles Kinbote: The author of the long series of notes that accompany John Shade's poem. He is thrilled to live near Shade, for he hopes that the poet will become enraptured by his stories about Charles the Beloved and write poems about them.

Odon (Donald O'Donnell): An actor and a friend of Charles the Beloved. Odon helps Charles escape from Zembla. In America, Odon's mother, Sylvia, takes Charles in.

Hazel Shade: John Shade's daughter. As a child, Hazel is overweight and unpopular. She is cast in grotesque character parts in school plays. Once, a young man agrees to be her blind date, but after one look at Hazel, he bolts. Hazel drowns when she falls through the surface of an icy lake.

John Shade: A college professor and the author of the four-canto poem "Pale Fire." Shade is sixty-one years old and grateful for his wife's tender attentions to him. He funnels his frustrations into poetry. "Pale Fire" examines his life, his thoughts on eternity, the afterlife, his daughter's death, and his love for his wife. He is aware that Kinbote hopes he will incorporate tales about Charles the Beloved into his poem, but he refuses to be pressured by his persistent neighbor.

Sybil Shade: John Shade's wife. Sybil loathes her next-door neighbor, Charles Kinbote. She is suspicious of his demands on her husband's time. Whenever possible, she thwarts Kinbote's forays into the Shade house, but she is civil to Kinbote when she must be. In a moment of grief, grateful upon hearing the rumor that Kinbote threw himself in front of her husband in an attempt to save him, Sybil signs an agreement giving Kinbote sole editor's rights to her husband's last poem.

Pale Fire

Reading
Pale Fire

Foreword*

Charles Kinbote, who identifies himself as a devoted friend of the late poet **John Shade**, has written this Foreword as an introduction to his annotated edition of John Shade's last poem, "Pale Fire." Kinbote tells us that Shade used to transfer his final draft of each day's work to index cards. Kinbote says he now possesses these cards, which are, no matter what the so-called Shadeans say, a definitive final text. Kinbote also has a contract signed by Shade's widow, **Sybil**, granting Kinbote permission to annotate and publish Shade's poem. Sybil's lawyer has bitterly denounced Kinbote's publication plan, but Sybil's original permission stands.

Kinbote discusses the delay in publishing the poem and notes, blaming it on the mess surrounding Shade's death and a publisher who insisted on naming a co-editor for the poem. Kinbote also mentions "a jailed killer." There were also

---

* A Note on Structure: *Pale Fire* is comprised of a foreword, a poem in four cantos, and then lengthy notes meant to serve as commentary on the poem. For ease of discussion, this book analyzes each canto and its corresponding notes in succession.

95

Vladimir Nabokov

complications with the Shadeans and Sybil. Nonetheless, Kinbote worked diligently and triumphed. Kinbote has decided to position his commentary after the poem, not before it.

Kinbote explains that he probably knew Shade better than anyone else, which makes him the natural choice to annotate Shade's poem. He first saw Shade on a winter day, when Shade was having trouble with his car. Later, Kinbote was formally introduced to Shade in the faculty dining room. The colleagues jeered good-naturedly at Kinbote's confession that he was a vegetarian, and Shade said that for him, eating even one vegetable was an enormous effort. Kinbote recalls Shade's limping walk, ailing heart, and extraordinary gray hair.

A few days later, Kinbote offered Shade a ride home when Sybil was a minute late picking him up. Shade shrugged and accepted. Kinbote stopped to buy cookies and caviar, and Shade popped into a liquor store and returned smelling of brandy.

> "The substance of the book is in a long series of notes to the poem — notes designed to construct a whole imaginary world, with its population, customs, royal family, philosophy, social custom, flung together at the hazard of a line-by-line commentary."
>
> **GEORGE CLOYNE**, *THE NEW YORK TIMES*

During the following weeks, Kinbote spied on the Shades from his upstairs window as the poet and his wife went about their routine lives. It was a difficult time for Kinbote because, according to him, Shade preferred Kinbote's company to anyone else's, which made Kinbote's colleagues jealous. A young instructor snidely referred to Kinbote as the Great Beaver. Later, Kinbote was lampooned in a school skit as a woman-hater who munched raw carrots and quoted A.E. Housman (see page 38). The head of Kinbote's department summoned Kinbote and cautioned him to be "more careful." He was not referring to the recent rumors, but to the fact that Kinbote had called some of his colleagues mediocrities. Kinbote wonders whether the department head, along with Shade, knows something (about Kinbote, presumably) that only two trustees and the president of the college definitely know.

As for John Shade, Kinbote says, he was a very private person. His unkempt exterior was a way of dealing with his own imperfections, keeping the good on the inside and the bad on the outside. Kinbote treasures a photo of himself with Shade, who is leaning on his aunt's cane.

Kinbote hopes that his Foreword has not been too skimpy. He wants readers to appreciate the masterpiece that Shade left behind, as well as his own notes. He suggests that readers should consult the notes two or even three times to assist with their reading the poem. Better yet, readers might want to purchase two copies of the volume so that Shade's poem and Kinbote's notes can lie adjacent to one another. Without his notes, Kinbote says, the poem has absolutely no meaning.

UNDERSTANDING AND INTERPRETING
Foreword

On the Defensive: Throughout the foreword, Kinbote's tone is authoritarian and hotly defensive. No one, he continually emphasizes, is as qualified to edit this poem as he is. He claims he knew Shade better than anyone else did, although from the evidence we read in the Foreword, it seems that he was not a close friend of the poet's. From the beginning of the novel, then, we wonder if we can trust what Kinbote says. He claims his friendship with Shade was so mutually satisfying that it incited gossips to condemn Shade for preferring Kinbote's company to that of any of his other colleagues. It seems clear to us, however, that rumors about Kinbote were inspired by more than just this relationship with Shade. Kinbote also admits to a struggle with Sybil Shade and a pack of Shadeans, so we know that Kinbote's confidence in his own interpretive abilities is not shared by everyone.

All about Me: For a Foreword purporting to introduce a poem by Shade, Kinbote gives us little background about Shade or his work. Instead, he focuses largely on himself. The foreword contains lengthy stories and confessions about Kinbote and relegates John Shade to the background. Kinbote feels superior to Shade in some ways. For example, he points out that Shade drives an old Packard automobile, while he owns a powerful red car. Most of the time, however, Kinbote plays the wounded victim. Kinbote gets teased about his vegetarianism, gossiped about by faculty, and ridiculed by students. Alone, he has had to battle Sybil, her lawyer, and the Shadeans while trying to finish his labor of love. The focus of this foreword is on Kinbote, the victim, not on Shade, the author.

Affinities with *Lolita*: Like *Lolita*, this uniquely structured novel contains a foreword in which a fictional editor explains his methods and justifies his editorial decisions. In *Lolita*, John Ray, Jr., cites a decision of the honorable John M. Woolsey as a legal precedent; in *Pale Fire*, Kinbote explains his methods. John

Ray, Jr. explains how he came to edit Humbert Hubert's manuscript; Kinbote explains how he came to edit Shade's poem. The *Lolita* foreword mentions a jailed killer (Humbert); so does the *Pale Fire* foreword. Despite these similarities, however, we have a much more eccentric editor in *Pale Fire* than we do in *Lolita*. For example, Kinbote announces that he has decided not to place his notes before the poem itself, a decision he has made "in conformity with custom." It is odd that he portrays placing his footnotes before the poem as a possibility, since footnotes and annotations almost always follow or run alongside the original text, thereby giving the original text pride of place. Kinbote goes on to make the claim that no one can understand Shade's poem without having read his notes. He even says that people should read his notes *first*, before reading the poem. This suggestion denies the purpose of footnotes, which is to illuminate, but never give basic meaning to, the original text.

Lampooning Freudians: Here, as in *Lolita* and *Pnin*, Nabokov satirizes pretentious, shallow-minded academic professors and Freudian theorizing. Several incidents hint that Kinbote is a closeted homosexual. In a college skit, Kinbote is lampooned as a woman-hater who chomps on raw carrots and constantly quotes Housman. The Housman in question is **A.E. Housman** (1859–1936), a closeted homosexual British poet. The skit further lampoons Kinbote's sexuality by portraying him eating raw carrots. Objects like carrots are, at least for Freudians, phallic symbols. With this cruel skit, Nabokov shows us the crudeness of Freudians and their ideas. He also points out the close-mindedness of some professors, showing us how Kinbote lives in fear of people discovering his sexual inclinations. Kinbote is relieved when the head of his department serves him a warning about verbal indiscretions. His relief suggests he was worried that the head planned to chastise him about his sexuality.

Canto One

POEM

In Canto One, Shade writes that he was "the shadow of a waxwing," a bird, that flew into a windowpane. As the shadow of the bird, he survived and flew away to "duplicate" other things—an apple, a lamp, even himself. The snow during the night turned to frost in the morning, and bird tracks are discovered on the snow.

Colors delighted him. Long ago, he could see his front porch from the lake, but today, he cannot see it, although he does not know why. His favorite tree is now large and rough-barked, and "white butterflies turn lavender" as they fly through it. He sees a lingering ghost of his daughter's old swing. His house is similar to the way it was long ago, though the solarium, picture window, chairs, and television set are new.

When Shade was an infant, his parents died. Both of them were experts on birds. He has reclaimed them so often in memory that he now possesses the equivalent of "a thousand parents," always dissolving into two phrases: "bad heart" and "cancer of the pancreas." Shade was reared by his aunt Maud, who painted "realistic objects interlaced with grotesque" ones. Shade and his wife have kept Maud's room intact.

Shade recalls hearing crickets at night and seeing the Great Bear in the sky. When he looked at the sky, he saw the realm of time that can close its wings and kill you. Those who do not look up when they walk, and only see the Milky Way while urinating, are better off.

As a child, Shade was "asthmatic, lame, and fat." He was only the shadow of a dead waxwing bird. When he was eleven, he was watching one of his wind-up toys when he suffered a sudden "sunburst" in his head and then everything went black. Although he recovered, the "wonder . . . and the shame" are still with him.

NOTES

In his lengthy notes to Canto One, Charles Kinbote furnishes details about the waxwing, explaining its size and coloring. He has seen many waxwings in New Wye, where he lived next door to John Shade. A bird resembling a waxwing appears on the royal coat of arms of Charles the Beloved of Zembla, a deposed king who has suffered innumerable misfortunes. On the day Shade began the poem, Kinbote was playing chess with a young Iranian. Four days later, a man named **Gradus** departed from Zembla, bent on murdering King Charles.

Kinbote extracts single words and phrases from the poem to support his conviction that Shade intended to fill his long poem with the sad but glorious history of Charles the Beloved. Shade would have done so, Kinbote is convinced, had it not been for the censorious editing of Shade's villainous wife, **Sybil**. And yet, argues Kinbote, a sufficient number of clues to Shade's original intention still exist to reconstruct what Shade intended for his poem.

Regretting that only occasional slivers of King Charles's epic life story remain in the poem, Kinbote relates some of the particulars in full. The king's reign was peaceful and elegant. Even the weather was better under his reign. Education flourished. King Charles himself was so learned that he often donned a disguise and taught apple-cheeked lads the intricacies of James Joyce's *Finnegans Wake*

SHADES OF DANTE

In the *Inferno*, a poem in thirty-three cantos by Dante Alighieri (1265–1321), Dante continually refers to the spirit of Virgil, who accompanies Dante on his journey through Hell. Virgil takes the form of a shade during his journey, and all the dead souls in Hell are referred to as shades. From childhood on, John Shade has felt that he is a shade, a shadow. In his poem, he portrays himself as the shade of the waxwing slain, and in life he seems to be a shade of his dynamic wife. He may think of himself as a shadow of his former self.

in the local school. Kinbote writes that the word "gray" in line 29 of Shade's poem undoubtedly refers to the assassin Gradus, a man with many pseudonyms: Jakob Gradus, Jack Degree, Jacques de Grey, James de Gray and sometimes merely Ravus. The phrase "frozen stillicide" evokes, says Kinbote, the idea of regicide.

Shade's discussion of his "frame house" inspires Kinbote to discuss the house that he rented near the Shades' house. The family photographs hanging on the walls were so repugnant that he replaced them with a reproduction of an early Picasso work featuring a naked lad leading a horse. The owner had, surprisingly, left behind notes with many instructions, including a complicated weekly menu for the house cat, which Kinbote ignored. Shade used to visit Kinbote's rented house and laugh with him at its owner's eccentricities. One day, Sibyl told Kinbote that Shade was working on a new poem, adding that Shade never let anyone read his work until he was finished.

To glimpse Shade at work, Kinbote began to spy on Shade using binoculars and even peeping in the windows. On one occasion, while sneaking in the back door, he interrupted Shade reading a section of his poem to his wife. Kinbote was jealous because he had been denied just such a recital. At home, Kinbote spent sleepless nights wishing that Shade would suffer a heart attack, and Kinbote might be called on to comfort him.

Kinbote mentions some lines of Shade's that were never used in the final draft. In these lines, Kinbote is sure that he can see poetic reflections of a tale that he told Shade about the King of Zembla fleeing in outlandish garb, aided by hundreds of loyal impersonators who dressed like him to confuse the revolutionaries out to depose him. Kinbote is convinced that Sybil excised those passages. He mentions and discounts a brief biography of Shade in a literary magazine, saying it has unforgivable inaccuracies.

Shade's use of the word "parents" prompts Kinbote to discuss the parents of Charles, King of Zembla. Charles' father was a bumbling king fascinated by mechanics, and his mother died of an obscure blood ailment. Young Charles was especially close to Otar, a cultured lad with a large nose. A girl tried unsuccessfully to seduce Charles, who dreamed of a horde of handsome pageboys bursting into his bedroom. Many years later, Charles married a woman named **Disa**.

Kinbote is ecstatic when he finds mention of "a secret corridor" in one of Shade's discarded lines. He says this is obviously a reference to Charles the Beloved's escape from his in-house imprisonment, where he awaited probable murder at the hands of the revolutionaries. As a youth, Charles had discovered a secret passage, which he explored with a young friend. Years later, Charles escaped from his jailers using this secret corridor and then took refuge in a cave near a beach.

THE SIBYL OF CUMAE

In Virgil's *Aeneid*, the Sibyl of Cumae is Aeneas's guide in the Underworld. Hoping the Sibyl will permit him to have his way with her, the Greek god Apollo offers her anything she wishes. She asks for as many birthdays as grains of sand in her hand, thinking she is making a clever wish. Her wish is granted, but because the Sibyl wished for age without eternal youth, she becomes hideous. As the years pass, she ages and withers away until she is barely more than a voice. Nabokov links Sybil Shade to Aeneas's Sibyl by making their names homonyms and by mentioning Sybil's aging process— although Sybil, unlike the Sibyl of Cumae, is untouched by the passage of time, at least in her husband's eyes.

UNDERSTANDING AND INTERPRETING
Canto One and Commentary

A Mediocre Poem: The poem "Pale Fire" is not remarkable, nor is it meant to be. The comedy of this novel is that a slight, mediocre poem, which probably has only one meaning, is overloaded with commentary and notes that generously assign nonexistent depths and meaning to the poem. In the character of Kinbote, Nabokov satirizes poets' colleagues who have no talent for composing poems themselves and so become literary critics of their peers, scribbling verbose, convoluted interpretations that are more about themselves than the primary work that they purport to critique. Shade's poem is middling, not bad. It shows sensitivity, and appeals with its soft alliteration and modesty. It also contains some ambiguous passages, and it is these and others that Kinbote uses to expound on the story of Charles the Beloved, the last king of Zembla.

Kinbote's Manipulation: Kinbote rarely analyzes the poem as it relates to Shade's life or Shade himself, even though the poem is clearly autobiographical. Instead, Kinbote uses Shade's poem to talk about himself and Charles the Beloved. Single words are taken out of context and used to justify extended recollections of Charles' escapades—his childhood games, his adolescent sexual delights with other youths, and his weary willingness to suffer the flirtations of a girl named Fleur.

Kinbote versus Sybil Shade: Kinbote's relationship with Sybil Shade is pivotal, and it is immediately obvious that they are rivals. She is possessive of her husband and resents Kinbote's attempts to spend time with him. For Kinbote, however, Shade is the ideal repository for his history of Charles the Beloved. Kinbote wants to kidnap Shade's work and force it to tell the story of Charles the Beloved. He becomes obsessed with Shade, defying Sybil and becoming a voyeur, peering into the Shade house.

Forcing Immortality: In *Lolita*, Humbert is obsessed by his longing to possess Lolita. His rival is Lolita's mother, Charlotte Haze. In *Pale Fire*, Kinbote is obsessed with his story of Charles the Beloved. His rival is Sybil. Humbert never manages to gain an emotional hold over Lolita, so he writes his memoir to capture her in words and to immortalize their story. *Lolita* is not as much about the girl of its title as it is about Humbert. Similarly, Kinbote cannot gain a hold over Shade, so he writes the notes to Shade's poem in order to immortalize his own story of Charles the Beloved. *Pale Fire* is not primarily about John Shade or his poem, but about Charles the Beloved and Kinbote.

Canto Two

POEM

Canto Two concerns Shade's daughter, Hazel. As a prelude, Shade recalls that when he was a child, he thought adults knew all there was to know about the afterlife. Now, at sixty-one, he wonders how people manage to live without some assurance of life after death. His Aunt Maud was eighty when she suffered a massive stroke. Afterward, she had to battle the monsters in her brain and struggle for words. Perhaps she should have died. Perhaps after death, we can converse with Proust or talk with Socrates. Why not believe in such an afterlife when no one truly knows what lies beyond the grave?

Shade says his wife, Sybil, is immune to Time's ravages. They met on a senior class trip to New Wye Falls, and he still remembers how beautiful she was. Forty years later, he still finds her beautiful.

Hazel was not blessed with her mother's beauty, but Shade and Sybil rationalized her unattractiveness as merely an awkward phase. Hazel was left out of games and in school plays, she was made to play Mother Time or a cleaning woman, while her playmates played elves and fairies.

Shade wept in the school bathroom for his daughter. Instead of going on dates, Hazel was sent abroad by her parents. At college, she was solitary. Her roommate became a nun. Hazel spent three mysterious nights in an old barn, where she observed the lights and sounds. One night, Hazel had a blind date with a boy named Pete, a cousin of Shade's typist. The typist, the typist's fiancé, and Hazel went to pick up Pete, who immediately pretended he had just remembered a previous engagement. Hazel said she understood, and caught a bus home. Hazel got off the bus and started walking across a frozen lake. The ice broke, and she drowned. Some say she lost her way. Others say she took her own life.

NOTES

Kinbote continues to chronicle the adventures of Charles the Beloved after his successful escape from Zembla. A vengeful group of revolutionaries, the Shadows, chose an obscure man named Gradus to find and kill Charles. By coincidence, Gradus was chosen on the very night that Shade penned the first lines of "Pale Fire." Kinbote supposes that a draw of cards must have decided Gradus's mission, for Gradus was by nature a bumbler. The Shadows caught a man who turned out to be one of Charles's many impersonators. A committee that included Gradus decided to kill the impersonator, but the firing squad failed to execute him. While the victim was in the hospital recuperating, Gradus again attempted, and failed, to kill him.

Kinbote mentions Shade's low opinion of Professor Pnin, the demanding head of the Russian department. Kinbote says that Shade believed poetry, not ideas or social background, is what matters. Students should "get drunk on the poetry of *Hamlet* and *King Lear.*" Kinbote asked whether Shade actually approved of Shakespeare's "purple passages." Shade responded by saying that he rolls on them as joyfully as a mongrel does on a Great Dane's feces.

Kinbote tells of Gradus's landing in Copenhagen. He mentions a young friend of his who needed a ride and had no license. Kinbote chauffeured him 200 miles and accompanied him to a party. The next day, upon finding his car in a pine grove, he was furious to find it contained swimming trunks and "a girl's silver slipper." He sought out his gardener for a massage before seeking out Shade's company.

Sybil had other plans. She was hosting a birthday party for Shade, and Kinbote was not invited. Kinbote drank all alone in his house, watching the guests arrive from his window. The next morning, after Sibyl had gone out, Kinbote went to the Shades' bearing an extravagant dressing gown as a present for the poet. He noticed a stack of books, mostly by Faulkner, by the garage. At that moment, Sybil returned and assured Kinbote that she had saved him from the tedium of the previous night's party. Kinbote retaliated, saying yesterday was his birthday, too. He was born sixteen years after Shade. He gave Sybil the final volume of Proust's *Remembrance of Things Past,* with pages 269–271 marked. These pages detail a social slight in which Mme. de Mortemart venomously neglects to invite Mme. de Valcourt to her party and afterward explains herself using almost exactly the same words that Sybil Shade just used.

In the meantime, Kinbote tells us, Gradus left Copenhagen for Paris. Shade's words "a domestic ghost" in line 230 remind Kinbote that Shade's typist told him how poltergeists plagued the Shades, making chairs walk in and out of rooms, plates fly, saucepans crash, and snowballs appear in the icebox. According to the typist, Shade was frightened that Hazel had triggered the appearance of these spirits.

Kinbote continues the story of Charles the Beloved and Disa, the woman Charles the Beloved eventually married. When Charles first saw Disa, she looked divine. She came to a costume party dressed as a young male stripling, flanked

PROUST AT PARTIES

Marcel Proust (1871–1922), a Modernist French writer, was plagued with ill health and spent a good deal of time lying in bed and writing. When Proust judged himself well enough to attend parties, he made bountiful mental notes about the postures, niceties, and neuroticisms he observed.

His masterpiece, *Remembrance of Things Past*, contains gossip and social chit-chat, reflecting and satirizing the status-conscious men and women of his social milieu. Kinbote hands Sybil Shade a copy of Proust's final volume with a passage marked to show her that he knows what game she plays.

by two good-looking male cousins. Two years later, when Disa was twenty-one years old, Charles proposed to her. His advisors had been pleading for him to produce an heir.

Kinbote returns to the story of Gradus, who landed in Paris and tried to find the exiled King. Because he was not clever enough, Gradus did not try to pass himself off as a Charles loyalist, and was accused of being a snooping Danish reporter. Kinbote adds that Sybil is not as clever as she thinks she is. She hoped to whisk Shade away to a secret location, but Kinbote talked to Shade's doctor and found out that they were headed for an American mountain range. He hoped to surprise Shade by suddenly popping out from behind a boulder, garbed in Tirolese attire. Kinbote then examines line 334's phrase "[w]ould never come for her" and adds that he was often lonely, waiting for a young friend or for John Shade.

Kinbote explains Gradus's scheme to meet Joseph S. Lavender in order to discover the whereabouts of King Charles. A bronzed, well-built teenager in a scanty loincloth escorted Gradus toward the pool. They passed a rustic out-door toilet. On the door was scribbled, "The King was here." At the pool, the young Adonis doffed his loincloth and lay on his back in the sun. Gradus left in disgust.

Kinbote rails against Shade's poetic adoration of his wife. She was an old woman well over sixty-one when Shade wrote those glowing words about her. The truth is that the woman Shade describes in his poem sounds not like Sybil, but like Disa. Kinbote then tells us about Charles' early years with Disa. Charles was not attracted to her, but one night, aphrodisiacs inspired him to propose sex. The manner in which he wanted to have sex repulsed Disa. Charles went on a cruise with his friends. For a while, he tried to resist the temptation of young men, but his resolve slipped, first occasionally, then several times daily, especially with Harfar, an enormously endowed young man. In time, Disa retired to a villa on the Riviera.

UNDERSTANDING AND INTERPRETING
Canto Two and Commentary

Our Suspicious Annotator: Although Canto Two is almost wholly about Hazel, Kinbote's notes do not reflect it. He jumps about from subject to subject, detailing his hatred of Sybil and continuing the harrowing saga of King Charles. He relates stories about the assigned assassin, Gradus, that he could

DIS

Nabokov names the wife of Charles the Beloved "Disa," which is a feminine form of "Dis," the city of the Underworld in Greek mythology and in Dante's *Inferno*. Disa is aptly named, since the thought of having sex with a woman is painful punishment for Charles. Charles must choose a bride so he can reproduce, so he chooses a woman who resembles, at least on their first meeting, a beautiful boy. Charles prays fervently for marital success before the wedding ceremony, but finds he cannot consummate the marriage and consign himself to Disa, his own female underworld.

not possibly know—unless Kinbote himself is the assassin. Nabokov makes us question Kinbote's identity and trustworthiness. We wonder how Kinbote knows as much about Gradus as he knows about Charles the Beloved.

Kinbote's Boys: Nabokov caricatures Kinbote as a nervous, naïve predator of young boys. Kinbote is continually on the lookout for attractive boys, luring them to his basement with two ping-pong tables. He contemplates adding a third for a young man who seems worthy of his own table. This young man, however, turns out to be straight—sexual treason in Kinbote's eyes. Kinbote is grateful, at least, for his gardener, who provides him with delicious rubdowns when the stress becomes too great. Kinbote uses the phrase "briefer than a girl's," a reference to a poem by A.E. Housman. (Humbert Humbert used this phrase in *Lolita* to refer to the brief span of a nymphet's beauty; see page 38.) Kinbote, who was lampooned in a college skit for his affinity with Housman, here links himself to the homosexual poet by referring to boys' brief garlands. When Gradus arrives at the villa of Joe Lavender, he is greeted by a young man who, according to Kinbote, is a "slender but strong-looking lad of fourteen or fifteen dyed a nectarine hue by the sun . . . [with] nothing on save a leopard-spotted loincloth." Kinbote revels in such descriptions. In Canto One, he was fairly discreet in his allusions to young men, but in Canto Two, he casts all discretion aside. Kinbote is like a homosexual double of Humbert Humbert, although his fixation on boys is not nearly as obsessive, disquieting, or monogamous as Humbert's fixation on girls. We already know that Kinbote is gay, and now it becomes clear that Charles the Beloved is, too. Charles' obsession with young men is comic. He lusts for the woman he marries only when he is hopped up on aphrodisiacs or when she is dressed as a boy. Charles cannot keep his hands off young men, and when he does finally marry in order to produce an heir, he fails to consummate the marriage.

Sybil Consumes Kinbote: Shade devotes part of this Canto to the beauty of his wife, Sybil. Kinbote uses Shade's praise of Sybil as an opportunity to lash out at her. He calls Shade's description of Sybil absurd, saying that Sybil is an old woman, a few months older than Shade himself, and she has not kept her youthful looks. If anything, Kinbote says, Shade has described the brave Disa, estranged wife of Charles the Beloved. Kinbote attacks Sybil's looks simply because he dislikes Sybil. Even Kinbote's seeming triumphs show his weakness, for they reveal how fully his obsession with the Shades consumes him. Sybil did not invite Kinbote to Shade's birthday party, but Kinbote says he won that battle by giving Shade a birthday gift and handing Sybil a Proustian put-down. We see, however, that this small triumph does not make up for the pain that Sybil caused Kinbote by shutting him out of the party. He suffered colossal anxiety through the night, rushing from window to window in hopes of glimpsing the party and the partygoers. Kinbote again thinks he wins by ferreting out the location of the Shades' escape, but actually he puts himself at Sybil's mercy. Her plans consume him, and he can think of nothing but following her and her husband.

Subtly Funny: Humor, sometimes in subtle form, fills *Pale Fire*. Someone named Professor Pnin makes a walk-on appearance as a martinet in the Russian department (in Nabokov's novel *Pnin*, Pnin is just the opposite—a sweet, ineffectual professor in a non-existent Russian department). Disa's full name is Disa, Duchess of Payn, and in enduring marriage to Charles the Beloved she becomes a sort of duchess of pain ("Payn" being, of course, a homonym for "pain"). On the estate of Joe Lavender, the outhouse door is decorated with the phrase *The King was here,* which recalls the WWII graffito "Kilroy Was Here," a mark of America's imprint on the world.

Canto Three

POEM

Shade recalls teaching at the Institute of Preparation for the Hereafter (I.P.H.), lecturing on "the Worm" of death. Sybil and little Hazel moved with him from New Wye to another state higher in the snow-capped mountains. Shade wondered if perhaps moving literally higher toward heaven might help him understand the mysteries of life, death, and the hereafter. Initially, what he realized was that from the day of our birth, we are on the road to death. Death does not thrive on the aged, but on the "blood-ripe" lives of youth. Our dearest experiences become crossed-out names in dog-eared address books. In the next life, he says philosophically, he is ready to become a small, modest flower or a fly.

He says he will "turn down eternity" unless it contains both the minor and the major matters of life—the red taillight of an airplane, Sybil's gesture of panic at running short of cigarettes, the way she smiles at dogs, the trail of slime left behind by a snail.

At I.P.H., students learned that it was wise not to expect too much beyond the grave. Perhaps one's soul will be tossed into a void. Students were instructed on how to act if they discovered themselves sailing through solid, earthly bodies or found themselves turned into a toad on a street. They discussed the possibility of meeting successive spouses after death.

Sybil remarked that she could not tell the difference between I.P.H. and Hell. It was likely that the institute declined when Freudians were allowed in. Shade considers that maybe his stint at I.P.H. prepared him for the sudden death of Hazel. He rationally understood that Hazel was lost to him forever, yet he and Sybil winced at night whenever they heard a strange sound. Shade's deep grief made him ready to believe in the impossible—the return of his beloved child. He and Sybil went to Italy for a time, and when they returned, Shade found himself "universally acclaimed." That fall, Hurricane Lolita swept havoc from Florida to Maine. Then one night, Shade died, in a manner of speaking.

The Cranshaw Club had paid him to discuss the meaningfulness of poetry, and after the talk, his heart seemed to stop. He remembers seeing a "rubber" sunset, and, in the dark void, a "tall white fountain." Then the vision melted away, and he was back on earth. Shade's doctor laughed at these visions. "Not dead" was the doctor's verdict, despite Shade's protests that he had briefly died. Later, Shade stumbled upon a magazine article about a woman whose heart had stopped and was massaged back to life by an attending physician. She later told an interviewer that she had seen, among other things, a tall white fountain.

Shade was stunned. He obtained Mrs. Z's address and drove 300 miles to talk to her. She gushed about meeting such an accomplished poet and brushed aside Shade's questions about her vision. Later, Shade called on Coates, the man who interviewed Mrs. Z. Coates pulled out his interview notes and discovered that Mrs. Z. said that she saw a tall, magnificent *mountain*, not a fountain. Shade concludes that the great answers to life come down to a misprint. It is all chance without reason or justice. Shade rushes to tell Sybil his conclusion, but she seems distracted.

NOTES

Kinbote thinks Shade is mistaken in his attitude toward God and the hereafter, in both of which Kinbote believes. Kinbote refers to Shade's words "the other" in line 579 and says that there was one young woman who might have tempted Shade, although he does not think Shade commited adultery.

The Shades invited Kinbote to their house three times, and he invited them to his house twelve times. They accepted only three times. He recalls his final meal with the Shades. Kinbote brought Shade a layout of King Charles's palace, and he was asked to stay for lunch. Sybil knew that Kinbote was a vegetarian, but she contaminated the salad greens with animal matter. When the Shades came to his house, he built his dinners around a single vegetable. Sybil whined that she was allergic to everything in the vegetable kingdom that began with the letter "a." Kinbote adds that no old dullards attended his dinners. Instead, he invited his gardener, the son of a Middle Eastern potentate, and, as an experiment, the girl with whom Shade was rumored to be having an affair.

Kinbote finds an instance in "Pale Fire" where the end of a word and the beginning of the following word spell out "gradus." It happened that as Shade wrote this puzzle, Gradus found out that he would be flying to Nice.

Kinbote returns to the flight of King Charles from Zembla. Charles would have perished had he not listened to his premonitions, but Kinbote is certain that even if the king had been caught, he would have spit in the eye of his executioners. Kinbote comments that Cedarn, from where he is writing these notes, has become a ghost town. He recalls a woman at a cocktail party asking him to comment on a man who thought he was God. The woman said he was a loony, but Shade said the fellow was a poet.

> "It would be tedious to tabulate all the theories about who invented whom in *Pale Fire*. The central question is, as Humpty Dumpty puts it, 'Which is to be master.'"
>
> **MAURICE COUTURIER**, *THE GUARDIAN*

Kinbote glosses Shade's reference to Goethe's "Erlkönig," a poem about the erlking, who, in Kinbote's interpretation, "falls in love" with the son of a night traveler. The last King of Zembla, says Kinbote, treasured Goethe's lines about the erlking and chanted them to himself as he escaped from the Shadows.

Kinbote wonders why Shade gave a hurricane the Spanish name *Lolita* instead of a simple Anglo-Saxon name like *Linda* or *Lois*. Spaniards sometimes call their parrots "Lolita." In his next note, Kinbote says it is wrong to think that all Russians are gloomy. He has personally known two cheery ones, Andronnikov and Niagarin, both handsome and manly. Kinbote is sure that Charles the Beloved has a good amount of dashing Russian blood.

By dramatic coincidence, Kinbote says, Shade's heart attack coincided with Charles the Beloved's arrival in America. Charles parachuted from a chartered plane into a field. He was still struggling with the parachute when a Rolls-Royce from Sylvia O'Donnell's manor drove up, complete with a British chauffeur and scotch. Sylvia, the mother of Charles's friend, **Odon**, had also sent along an article about Shade's heart attack and hospitalization. Charles was immediately interested, because Shade was his favorite American poet.

Reclining in bed, Sylvia greeted Charles and said that she was preparing for a sojourn in Africa. She asked about her son, who was said to be living with a notorious actress. Charles assured her that Odon promised he would never marry this woman. Sylvia jangled a small bell, and a male attendant entered bearing fruit. Sylvia advised Charles to forget about the attendant, who is straight. She cautioned him that he would have to be more careful about satisfying his sexual appetite. She rented a lovely house for him, next door to the Shades.

We now realize that Charles Kinbote and King Charles the Beloved are the same man. When Kinbote/Charles the Beloved later meets Shade, the poet explains that his heart attack was not the emergency that it seemed at first. This reevaluation, according to Kinbote, does not undermine the power of the passage in Shade's long poem describing his half-stilled heart.

In the meantime, Gradus has landed in Nice. Kinbote knows that the bumbler Gradus was so tortured by his ravenous libido that several times he attempted to castrate himself, failing each time. Gradus chances to read about a burglary at Disa's villa. Thieves made off with a jewel box and old medals. Shortly afterward, Gradus is told he will be going to New York. In Disa's jewel box was a letter from her husband, Charles the Beloved, revealing his pseudonym and his address in New Wye, Appalachia, USA.

UNDERSTANDING AND INTERPRETING
Canto Three and Commentary

Sybil, Sin, and Selfish Satisfaction: Kinbote blames almost everything that disturbs him, from Shade's spiritual beliefs to failed dinners, on Sybil. He worries about Shade's nonchalance about the afterlife. Kinbote believes that God has a presence in our lives and rules in the afterlife. Shade will not hear of that possibility. He has come to believe that all is chance and accident. Kinbote is sure that were it not for Sybil, Shade, with his naturally romantic and poetic soul, would envision the afterlife as spiritual and holy. Sybil is a lapsed, bitter Catholic, so it is little wonder that Shade had such difficulty describing man's condition in this life and the next. According to Kinbote, Sybil's perversion of Shade's innate spirituality borders on the satanic. Her perverseness extends even to the secular dinner that Kinbote hopes to have with the Shades. Sybil thwarts him by serving salad greens tainted with animal matter. Whenever Kinbote struggles and fails to find his own meaning in Shade's poem, he decides that Sybil has intervened, twisting Shade's poetry so that Kinbote cannot gain entrance to Shade's literary meaning. She alone knows Shade's secrets, she alone has the keys to the puzzles in his poem—and yet she refuses to share them with Kinbote. Kinbote is sure that she has hated him from the start because she believed he posed a threat to her relationship with her husband. When Kinbote first wrote to Shade, praising him as a worshipful fan might, he received no answer, which he takes as proof of Sybil's intervention.

The Pain of Non-Coincidence: Kinbote tries to make the movements of Charles the Beloved and Gradus the assassin line up with Shade's writing progress, a project that is both funny and pathetic. The parallels are never really there, and most painfully absent is the parallel Kinbote most longs for. He wants to believe that he (Charles the Beloved) parachuted into America at the very moment that Shade's soul left his body for a split second. Later, however, Shade assures Kinbote that he probably did not suffer a heart attack at all. His doctor is not convinced that his heart stopped. No mini-death occurred simultaneously with Charles's crash-landing in a Baltimore hayfield, no matter how much Kinbote longs for that coincidence.

> "This centaur-work of Nabokov's, half poem, half prose, this merman of the deep, is a creation of perfect beauty, symmetry, strangeness, originality, and moral truth. Pretending to be curio, it cannot disguise the fact that it is one of the very great works of art of this century, the modern novel that everyone thought was dead and that was only playing possum."
>
> **MARY MCCARTHY**, *THE NEW REPUBLIC*

Charles and the Boys: Nabokov continues to make fun of Kinbote's obsession with young boys. Kinbote seems unaware that his inclusion of all sorts of details about young men has absolutely no relevance to Shade's poem or even to his own narrative notes. When Charles speaks of youths preyed on by Death, he describes them as "blood-ripe," as if they are ready to eat. When he describes his dinner-party guests, he praises his young male guests and describes the single young woman invited as a freak with green-circled eyes. Kinbote is hilarious when he describes the young Russian men who disprove the stereotype that all Russians are gloomy. Kinbote describes, in great detail, their hair, their clean-cut jaws, their swaggers, their astonishing smiles, even their soft leather boots. Nabokov also sends up repressed America. When the jaded, world-weary Sylvia tinkles her bell to summon her handsome attendant, she warns Charles that the fellow is off-limits. Now that Charles is in America, she says, he must keep a low-profile and hide his sexual proclivities. America is a repressed, homophobic place, and Charles is no longer a king.

Error and Disenchantment: Shade believes that during his supposed heart attack, he was granted a vision of the afterlife, a subject he had taught for one term at the Institute of Preparation for the Hereafter. Initially, Shade believed that because no one knew anything definite about the afterlife, one might as well assume it existed, prepare for it, and think about the consequences of one's actions. For a full term, while at the I.P.H., he pondered such problems as meeting multiple spouses in heaven, the possibility of drifting in a void, and the various surprises one might encounter if suddenly reincarnated. The assumption behind these questions was that all one had to be concerned with was the entrance into afterlife and what happened after that. However, when Shade searches out the woman who had a near-death experience and supposedly saw a fountain, he is absolutely disillusioned. Because her experience, which resembled his own so closely, turns out to be nothing more than a misprint, Shade concludes that there is no single afterlife and that the total meaning of life turns out to be nothing.

Canto Four

POEM

Shade discusses the composition of poetry—composition in the mind and composition with pen in hand. Thoughts filter through the pen, which is almighty and can erase a sunset or restore a star that was initially crossed out. Shade prefers composing on midsummer mornings when he is half-awake and not sure what is real and what is unreal.

Shade imagines a biographer writing that he (Shade) is like a king while shaving in the bath, and yet, like Marat (a French revolutionary who was stabbed to death while bathing), he bleeds. Unlike the suave shaver on TV who shaves in a flourish, Shade shaves with many meticulous strokes. He speaks of things he loathes: jazz, Spanish matadors, abstract art, folk masks, progressive schools, supermarket music, swimming pools, "brutes," "bores," Freud, Marx, cocky poets, and fakes.

Shade speaks of his muse and of Sybil. His muse is with him always, just as Sybil is. Sybil is youth, and it delights him when she quotes his poems and makes them new again. This day has passed with a "low hum of harmony." His brain feels drained, and finally he feels as though his art has helped him fathom existence, or at least a small bit of his own existence. In the distance, he hears the clang of horseshoes being tossed. A dark Vanessa butterfly flies as the sun sets. Shade notes that he sees a neighbor's gardener going by, pushing an empty wheelbarrow up the lane.

Vladimir Nabokov

NOTES

Kinbote ignores Shade's discussion of composition and speaks of Gradus. He also expresses regret that Shade did not choose him as his official biographer. In line 894, Shade mentions a king, which causes Kinbote to recall that people have often remarked on his likeness to Charles the Beloved. Kinbote modestly protests at these remarks, but one day in the faculty club, faculty members insisted on the resemblance. Shade disagreed, saying Kinbote looks nothing like the deposed monarch. A professor of physics, flaunting his knowledge of Soviet works such as *Dr. Zhivago*, said that "history has denounced" Charles. Shade countered that, in time, history would denounce all of them. He heard that the king had fled the country dressed in red.

Meanwhile, Gerald Emerald, a young instructor who once referred to Kinbote as a Great Beaver, fetched a picture of Charles the Beloved. Young Emerald protested that Kinbote could not possibly be Charles because Charles was "young, handsome . . . wearing a fancy uniform," and looked like a "fancy pansy." Kinbote was outraged.

Kinbote remembers laughing with Shade over a so-called learned work on American psychoanalysis, based on Freudian theories. One of the entries insisted that Red Riding Hood's red cap is a symbol of menstruation. Kinbote is surprised that Shade mentions Zembla only once, in passing, over the course of his poem. Why did Shade speak of shaving when he could easily have rhapsodized about Charles instead?

Gradus arrived in New York. He read the paper and learned that an apartment house was hit by a thunderbolt that smashed into a TV set and injured two people. He had a boy shine his shoes and then lunched on "pinkish pork." Gradus, waxy-skinned and unshaven, went to catch a plane to New Wye.

Upon arrival in New Wye, Gradus had violent diarrhea. He bumped into Gerald Emerald, who offered to take Gradus to the street he sought. Meanwhile, Shade and Kinbote were talking on the Shades' porch. Shade had finished his poem, and Kinbote suggested that they celebrate by opening a bottle of fine Tokay wine. Shade readily agreed. The two men went to Kinbote's house. Ostensibly to relieve Shade of his burden, Kinbote took possession of the fat envelope filled with index cards chronicling, Kinbote hoped, the reign of Charles the Beloved.

Kinbote tells of how he hired his gardener. Kinbote had seen him working shirtless at someone's house and stopped to talk. The gardener explained that for two years he was a nurse in a hospital for black people in Maryland. He hoped someday to "study landscaping, botany, and French." Kinbote promised him financial assistance. The next day, the gardener began working on the grounds of Kinbote's rented house. The muscular young black man was completely impotent, but he was muscular, and Kinbote loved to watch him work.

Kinbote and Shade saw Gradus ring Kinbote's doorbell. Kinbote whispered, "I will kill him." Then, Gradus fired his gun. His first bullet ripped a button from Kinbote's blazer. The second bullet whizzed past his ear. One of the bullets pierced Shade's heart. At that moment, the gardener's spade slammed into Gradus's head, and Gradus crumpled.

Kinbote called the police. Policemen and an ambulance arrived and took Gradus away, assuring him that they would take care of his head wound. At that moment, Dr. Sutton's daughter drove up with Sybil Shade. At daybreak the next day, Kinbote began reading the index cards containing Shade's poem. There was little mention of Zembla and none of Charles the Beloved. He snarled and read faster. Nothing. Kinbote says he cannot fully express the agony he felt. The poem was only an ordinary autobiographical Appalachian narrative, "beautifully written" but devoid of all mention of Zembla and Charles. Later, Kinbote reread it, liking it a bit better. Sybil heard that Kinbote threw himself between her husband and the murderer. She wanted to repay him for his bravery, and granted him permission to be editor and commentator for the poem.

Kinbote visited Gradus in prison, but eventually the failed assassin slit his throat with a safety razor blade. Gradus committed suicide, Kinbote concludes, because he could no longer live with the knowledge that he was a bungler. Before Kinbote left for Cedarn, in Utana, where he had hoped to vacation with the Shades, he sewed Shade's index cards in the pockets of a coat. Now he has finished his commentary. As for his future, he may assume other disguises, or he may turn up on another college campus as a happy heterosexual Russian, a writer in exile, or he may get in touch with Sylvia's son and with him produce a movie about the escape of Charles the Beloved. Or he may end up huddled and groaning in a madhouse.

UNDERSTANDING AND INTERPRETING
Canto Four and Commentary

The Relentless Advance: Like a film narrator counting down the moments until the murder, Kinbote keeps us apprized of exactly where Gradus is, where his next stop will be, and where Shade and Kinbote are as he makes his progress. The effect is similar to hearing a clock slowly ticking away the hours until the preordained moment of death. Nabokov chronicles Gradus's advance not just with suspense, but with humor. Gradus, paying serious attention to having his shoes polished, fails to note that the pork he is eating is underdone and wastes precious moments dealing with his diarrhea. Nabokov is writing about the murder of a man, but he does not hesitate to inject some scatological humor into the narrative.

The Role of Chance: Kinbote's notes make it seem as though there is nothing that can prevent Gradus from attempting to kill Kinbote/Charles the Beloved, but this is not true. Chance still plays a role in the unfolding of events. On the morning of the planned assassination, Gradus reads an account of a thunderstorm that crashed into an apartment building and injured two people. Something similar to the chance thunderstorm happens when Gradus attempts to shoot Kinbote. He misses several times, and one of the bullets kills Shade. It is by chance that Kinbote's gardener hears the shots and rushes to the front door, spade in hand, and hits Gradus over the head. The best-laid plans can go awry. Chance does determine the course of events, as Shade thought. The purest, most ironic proof of Shade's belief is his own chance death from a bullet meant for another man.

"*Pale Fire* is regularly interrupted, without any logical or stylistic transition, right in the middle of a sentence . . . . in the final chapter, a surprise awaits the reader. I am writing this in a hurry, have to correct exams, but I want to add that I am delighted with the book."

VLADIMIR NABOKOV
IN A LETTER TO JASON EPSTEIN

Disillusionment and Determination: After the murder, Kinbote waits until morning to read the four-canto masterpiece. He is crushed by his discovery that Shade's poem mentions Zembla only once in passing and does not mention Charles the Beloved at all. There is no mention of Charles's miraculous escape from the well-guarded palace by a secret corridor leading to the state theater, or of his actor friend who helped him, or of his flight over a treacherous mountain. Despite his disappointment, when Kinbote recovers from his shock that the poem contains nothing about Charles the Beloved, he realizes that he can still use the poem as a vehicle to record the fantastical adventures of himself/Charles the Beloved. This is especially true after Sybil signs papers giving him sole and exclusive rights to the editing and annotating of Shade's poem. Kinbote has not been bested, not by the rebels in Zembla, or by Shade's poem, or by the sinister Sybil.

Murder and Comedy: Even in a section of the novel concerned mostly with murder, Nabokov's humor does not flag. He brings Gerald Emerald back onstage as a key figure in the last chapter of Shade's life. Gerald earlier played the smart-mouthed mocker of Kinbote, and now he is the vehicle, literally, that takes Gradus to Kinbote's home. Kinbote dislikes young Emerald, and because of the young man, he is almost killed. In addition, Kinbote cites Hurricane Lolita, which devastated the coast from Florida to Maine. This reference is significant, since Shade's death occurs in 1959 and Nabokov's novel *Lolita* was published in the United States in 1958. The response to the novel was very much like a hurricane of howling, censorious voices, destroying the novel in one sense by vowing to prevent it from being sold or reviewed. Nabokov also mentions a rather foolish-sounding professor of physics who champions the novel *Dr. Zhivago*. This is another joke meant for faithful readers, for it was *Dr. Zhivago* that displaced *Lolita* on bestseller lists. Both novels were written by men whose first language was Russian. Finally, Nabokov takes a swipe at the Freudians by pointing out the absurdity of interpreting Little Red Riding Hood's cap as a symbol of menstruation.

Is Charles/Kinbote Mad? *Pale Fire* provokes a number of questions about its narrator. Is Kinbote a madman? Has he made up the entire history of Zembla? Does Zembla even exist? Does Shade exist, or has Charles Kinbote made him up and written the poem himself? These questions can be convincingly answered in a number of entirely different ways. They provide excellent fodder for theses. Whatever the state of Charles Kinbote's mind, one broad, almost obvious interpretation of *Pale Fire* is that the novel satirizes academics who write mediocre poems and the academics who write lengthy reviews of them and distort their meaning. *Pale Fire* is not a straightforward satire of academia, though, because its main character is a possible madman who produces an interpretation that itself coyly invites the interpretations of the very graduate students and professors it parodies.

The Index: The index, which follows Kinbote's notes, is an intricate cross-reference of the various characters and subject matter. It is noteworthy for its lack of any information about two of Kinbote's archenemies: Sybil Shade and Gerald Emerald.

Vladimir Nabokov

Conclusions

Nabokov's satire is both humorous and quite serious. When he taught in the U.S., Nabokov had no patience with the pretensions of his so-called intellectual colleagues. He found most of them pompous, vapid, and ineffectual as teachers. He also thought that they drank too much. In *Pale Fire*, he caricatures such academics but also makes them so believable that we became fond of them. We like Charles Kinbote and John Shade. Kinbote may be mad as a hatter, but that hardly matters. He is human, comic, a familiarly infuriating neighbor, and a riveting narrator.

SUGGESTIONS FOR FURTHER READING

Bell, L. Michael. "A Pninian Incident and an Item of Harvard Folklore." *Journal of Modern Literature* (Philadelphia, Pennsylvania), July 1986, 13:2, pp. 321–325.

Boyd, Brian. *Vladimir Nabokov: The American Years*. Princeton: Princeton University Press, 1991.

_____. *Vladimir Nabokov: The Russian Years*. Princeton: Princeton University Press, 1990.

_____. *Nabokov's* Pale Fire*: The Magic of Artistic Discovery*. Princeton: Princeton University Press, 1999.

Couturier, Maurice. "Nabokov's *Pale Fire*, or The Purloined Poem," *Revue Française d'Etudes Américaines*, no. 1 (April 1976).

Cowart, David. "Art and Exile: Nabokov's *Pnin.*" *Explicator* (Washington, D.C.), Fall 1988, 47:1, pp. 33–34.

Dennison, Sally: "Vladimir Nabokov: The Work of Art as Dirty Book." *Alternative Literary Publishing: Five Modern Histories*. Iowa City, Iowa: University of Iowa Press, 1984, pp. 157–189.

deVries, Gerard. "Squirrels." *The Nabokovian*, Fall 1987, 19, pp. 56–58.

Dupee, F.W. "*Lolita* in America." *Encounter* (London), 65, February 1959, pp. 30–35.

Field, Andrew. *Nabokov: His Life in Part.* New York: Viking Press, 1977.

Fraysse, Suzanne. "Worlds Under Erasure: *Lolita* and Postmodernism." *Cycnos*, v. 12, no. 2, 1995, pp. 93–100.

Garrett-Goodyear, J.H. "The Rapture of Endless Approximation': The Role of the Narrator in *Pnin.*" *Journal of Narrative Technique* (Ypsilanti, Michigan), Fall 1986, 16:3, pp. 192–203.

Haegert, John. "Artist in Exile: The Americanization of Humbert." *ELH* (Baltimore, Maryland), Fall 1985, 52:33, pp. 777–794.

Vladimir Nabokov

Hennard, Martine. "Playing a Game of Worlds in Nabokov's *Pale Fire*." *MFS: Modern Fiction Studies* (Baltimore, Maryland), Summer 1994, 40:2, pp. 299–317.

Hollander, John: "The Perilous Magic of Nymphets." *Partisan Review* (New York), 23 (4), Fall 1956, pp. 557–560.

Jackson, Paul R. "*Pale Fire*'s Counterfeit King." *Notes on Contemporary Literature* (Carrollton, Georgia), March 1984, 14:2, pp. 5–7.

Janeway, Elizabeth: "The Tragedy of Man Driven by Desire." *New York Times Book Review* (New York), August 17, 1958, pp. 5, 25.

Johnson, Donald Barton: "The Index of Refraction in Nabokov's *Pale Fire*." *Russian Literature TriQuarterly* (Ann Arbor, Michigan), 16, 1979, pp. 33–49.

Knapp, Shoshanna. "Hazel Ablaze: Literary License in Nabokov's *Pale Fire*." *Essays in Literature* (Malcomb, Illinois), Spring 1987, 14:1, pp. 105–115.

Nassar, Joseph. "Transformations in Exile: The Multilingual Exploits of Nabokov's Pnin and Kinbote." *Visible Language* 27, no. 1–2 (1993), pp. 253–272.

INDEX

Index

SPARKNOTES LITERATURE GUIDES